a Sunday Times series (No. 94)

Handbook for the

# FORD
# CORTINA

## MARK 1

**113E/114E and
118E/119E**

**SALOONS AND ESTATE CARS
from 1962**

------------------------------------------------------------

**PIET OLYSLAGER MSIA MSAE**

**NELSON**

Thomas Nelson and Sons Ltd
36 Park Street London WIY 4DE
PO Box 18123 Nairobi Kenya

Thomas Nelson (Australia) Ltd
597 Little Collins Street Melbourne 3000

Thomas Nelson and Sons (Canada) Ltd
81 Curlew Drive Don Mills Ontario

Thomas Nelson (Nigeria) Ltd
PO Box 336 Apapa Lagos

First published in Great Britain in 1963
Fourth edition 1968 (Manual No. 94)
Reprinted 1971
Reprinted 1974

ISBN 0 17 160094 0

Printed by Royal Vangorcum in The Netherlands.

# Contents

## SPECIAL NOTE

*Although every care is taken to ensure accuracy and completeness in compiling this book, no liability can be accepted for damage, loss or injury caused by any errors or omissions in the information given.*

# Preface

THIS MANUAL is intended to supplement (not to replace) the instruction book issued with the car by the manufacturer. It contains more detailed information on the maintenance and repair of the Cortina without being, or pretending to be, a fully comprehensive workshop manual.

The early sections of the book contain general information essential for both owner-driver and mechanic. They give full details about the models covered so that the reader does not have to refer to many different publications in order to find correct model designations, serial numbers, major modifications, prices, dimensions, lubrication, maintenance and other information.

The section *Repair Data* has been compiled and presented on the assumption that the reader knows something about repair work. Elementary procedures have therefore been omitted and the space has been devoted to more advanced information. Readers who are not qualified to carry out repairs and adjustments are strongly advised to leave them to official Ford dealers or distributors, whose mechanics possess special equipment and are fully informed about the latest modifications and design changes. Often it will be more economical to replace a component by either a new or a factory-reconditioned unit rather than attempt to repair it. In all cases of doubt it will pay to consult a dealer.

At the end of the book there are supplements dealing with the GT and Lotus versions of the Cortina, as well as a general engine fault finding chart.

PIET OLYSLAGER, MSIA, MSAE

Fig. 1. Consul Cortina, two-door Standard Saloon, 1962-64

Fig. 2. Cortina De Luxe, four-door Saloon, 1965-66

# FORD CORTINA

## General

### INTRODUCTION

The Ford Consul Cortina was introduced in September 1962 by the Ford Motor Company Limited, Dagenham, England, equipped with a 1·2 litre (1198cc) engine.

In January 1963 the Cortina Super with a 1·5 litre (1498cc), five-bearing-crankshaft engine, was announced to supplement the range. This engine became optionally available for the standard Cortina at the same time. Also introduced in 1963 were the 'Cortina-Lotus' (January) and the 'Cortina G.T.' (April). These models are not fully covered by this manual, but brief technical and adjustment data may be found on pages 66 and 68. The Standard models were discontinued in September 1965 and the remaining models were replaced by the new Cortina Mk. II range in October 1966 (UK), after a million Cortinas had been sold in four years. The Cortina 1200 Mk. I 1966 Model was continued in simplified form for some time by the Ford assembly plant in Amsterdam.

**Summary of models, with body type codes:**

| | 113E/114E 1198cc | 118E/119E 1498cc | First introduced |
|---|---|---|---|
| 2-door Standard: | 71 | 71 | Sept. 1962 |
| 4-door Standard: | 72 | 72 | Oct. 1962 |
| 2-door De Luxe, column change: | 73 | 73 | Sept. 1962 |
| 2-door De Luxe, floor change: | 74 | 74* | Sept. 1962 |
| 4-door De Luxe, column change: | 75 | 75 | Oct. 1962 |
| 4-door De Luxe, floor change: | 76 | 76 | Oct. 1962 |
| 2-door G.T. (118E/119E G.T.): | — | 77 | April 1963 |
| 4-door G.T. (118E/119E G.T.): | — | 78 | April 1963 |
| 2-door Super, column change: | — | 81 | Jan. 1963 |
| 2-door Super, floor change: | — | 82 | Jan. 1963 |
| 4-door Super, column change: | — | 83 | Jan. 1963 |
| 4-door Super, floor change: | — | 84 | Jan. 1963 |
| Estate Car De Luxe, column change: | 86 | 86 | March 1963 |
| Estate Car De Luxe, floor change: | 87 | 87 | March 1963 |
| Estate Car Super, column change: | — | 88 | March 1963 |
| Estate Car Super, floor change: | — | 89 | March 1963 |

*Also: 'Cortina developed by Lotus': 125E, from January 1963.
NOTE: 113E, 118E, and 125E are r.h.d., 114E and 119E are l.h.d. models.

### DESCRIPTION

The Ford Cortina was first produced in May, 1962, as a 2-door, five-passenger Saloon, available in Standard or De Luxe form. Pre-1965 models were known as 'Consul Cortina.'

The car is of conventional layout with independent front suspension by means of coil springs (McPherson), rigid rear axle with semi-elliptic leaf springs, a four-speed all-synchronized gearbox and an all-steel body of unitary construction.

Fig. 3. Consul Cortina Super, four-door Saloon, 1963-64

Fig. 4. Consul Cortina De Luxe Estate Car, 1963-64

Fig. 5. Cortina Super Estate Car, 1965-66

**Cortina Standard:**

Two- or 4-door Saloon, equipped with 1198 cc engine; rear axle 4·125 or 4·44:1; tyre size 5·20—13; 8 in diameter brake drums at the front; painted simplified radiator grille. Discontinued in September 1965.

*Interior:* Separate front seats; central, floor-mounted gear change and parking brake; rubber floor covering; ashtray; sun vizor on driver's side; single-tone finish.

*Factory-fitted optional extras:* Heater and demister, windscreen washers, white side-wall tyres, 1498 cc engine (from September 1964).

**Cortina de Luxe:**

As for Standard and in addition:

*Exterior:* Bright metal grille and body ornamentation, two-tone colour options.

*Interior:* Passenger's sun vizor; two ashtrays in rear compartment; hinged rear side windows (on 2-door models); door switch operated courtesy lights; temperature and oil pressure warning lights; glove box with lid; padded facia.

*Factory-fitted optional extras:* Bench-type front seat and column gear-change (up to September 1965); 1498 cc engine with 3·9 or 4·125:1 axle ratio; 9 in diameter brake drums at front; 5·60—13 tyres; coloured rubber floor covering. Automatic transmission (Borg-Warner, with 1498 cc engine, from December 1963).

**Cortina Super:**

Two- or 4-door Saloon with 1498 cc engine; rear axle 3·9 or 4·125 : 1; tyre size 5·60—13; 9 in diameter brake drums at front.

*Exterior:* Can be identified by the twin flashes along the waistline, bright metal window frames, aluminium wheel trims.

*Interior (as for de Luxe, and in addition):* Available with separate front seats and central floor-mounted gear-change and parking brake, or with bench-type front seat, column gear-change (up to September 1965) and parking brake under facia; looped pile carpet; two-colour seat trim; fresh-air heater; cigarette lighter.

*Factory-fitted optional extras:* Borg-Warner automatic transmission (from December 1963); white side-wall tyres.

**Estate Cars:**

Two models available: Estate Car de Luxe and Estate Car Super. For additional luggage accommodation the seat cushion can be folded forward through 180 degrees. Then fold the seat squab forward to complete the loading floor, which is accessible at the rear through a lift-up, counter-balanced tail-gate.

**Estate Car de Luxe:**

Five-door Estate Car, equipped with the 1198 cc engine; rear axle ratio 4·44 : 1; tyre size 6·00—13, 6-ply.

*Exterior:* Twin flashes along the waistline, bright metal window frames, aluminium wheel trims, two-tone colour.

*Interior:* As for Cortina de Luxe.

*Factory-fitted optional extras:* As for Cortina de Luxe. In addition: bright-metal side mouldings with or without two-tone paint.

**Estate Car Super:**

Five-door Estate Car, equipped with the 1498 cc engine; rear axle 3·9 or 4·125 : 1; tyre size 6·00—13, 6-ply.

*Exterior:* Side panels and tail-gate finished with Di-Noc imitation wood (from September 1965: chrome strips and duo-tone paint; 'Super' badges at rear of chrome strips).

**Fig. 6. Consul Cortina 1963, front compartment**

*Interior:* As for Cortina Super.
*Factory-fitted optional extras:* As for Cortina Super.

## IDENTIFICATION

**Engine number:**
The engine number is stamped at the right-hand side of the engine.

**Vehicle or chassis number:**
The vehicle number is located on a plate in the engine compartment on the battery side, and is prefixed by four characters, as follows (1962–64): First letter—assembly plant (Z—Dagenham, S—Southampton, etc.); two figures—body and gearshift

**Fig. 7. Cortina 1965, front compartment**

type (see *Summary of Models,* page 3); last letter—year of manufacture (1962: B, 1963: C, etc.). The serial number is suffixed by a letter indicating month of manufacture.

From January 1965: First letter—country, second letter—assembly plant, two figures—body type, next letter—year (1965: E, 1966: F), next letter—month.

## MODIFICATIONS

(See also under *Description*, pages 3–7)

**October 1963:**
1964 models introduced with circular instrument dials in binnacle above steering column, 'silent-shut' childproof locks (from September 1963), and omission of grease nipples ('greaseless chassis,' from July 1963).

**October 1964:**
1965 models introduced with the following modifications: 'Aeroflow' heating and ventilating system with positive air extraction at sides of rear window. Front wheel disc brakes ($9\frac{1}{2}$ in diameter). Pillar-mounted safety belt anchorages. Screen washers and heater standard equipment (all models except Standard). 'Dished' three-spoke steering wheel. Redesigned facia and controls (see Fig. 7). Redesigned radiator grille incorporating sidelamps and direction indicator flashers. More luxurious seats with better padding. Higher compression ratio, increased power output and torque. 'Cortina' instead of 'Consul' on bonnet badge. Twin radius arms on rear suspension of G.T. models.

**October 1965:** Standard saloons and steering column gearshift discontinued. Fixed front door ventilator windows (pivoting on export models). In outward appearance the 1966 models can be identified by the shape of the Aeroflow screens on the rear quarter panels, which now have a wider 'rim.' With the introduction of the Mk. II production of the Mk. I was discontinued, except for a simplified version of the 1200 for export to the Netherlands in CKD condition. This version differs from the 1966 models in the following: Only two-door available. Painted headlamp rims. Oval emblem on the right-hand front wing. Fixed front door vent panes. Different pattern on the vynil upholstery and rubber floor mat. No parcel shelf. No ash-trays in rear compartment. Panel lamp switch in the position of the wiper switch on 1965/66 models, the windscreen washer pump control is now combined with the wiper switch (as on the Mk. 11). Door trim panel of smooth material, except for the centre portion, which has four ribs bordered by two bright metal strips. The Aeroflow screens on the rear quarter panels are of grey plastic material. '1200' on left side of rear panel, beside number plate. As on the 1967 Mk. 11 models the brake master cylinder reservoir is also provided with a plastic extension to increase the fluid capacity which also serves to enable visual fluid level inspection without removing the filler cap.

## PRICES (U.K.)

Prices are ex-works, inclusive of Purchase Tax and are to the nearest pound (£).

|  | November 1962 | March 1963 | September 1964 | May 1965 | August 1966 |
|---|---|---|---|---|---|
| 2-door Standard, 1198cc: | 573 | 573 | 574 | 582 | — |
| 4-door „ „ : | 591 | 591 | 592 | 606 | — |
| 2-door De Luxe, 1198cc : | 597 | 597 | 598 | 630 | 659 |
| 4-door „ „ : | 616 | 616 | 617 | 654 | 683 |
| Estate Car (1198cc): | — | 683 | 684 | 733 | 776 |

| | November 1962 | March 1963 | September 1964 | May 1965 | August 1966 |
|---|---|---|---|---|---|
| 2-door Super, 1498 cc: | — | 670 | 671 | 690 | 720 |
| 4-door   „    „   : | — | 688 | 689 | 714 | 745 |
| Estate Car (1498 cc): | — | 786 | 787 | 817 | 849 |
| 2-door G.T., 1498 cc: | — | 749 | 750 | 769 | 800 |
| 4-door   „    „   : | — | 767 | 768 | 793 | 825 |
| 2-door Cortina-Lotus, 1558 cc: | — | 1100 | 992 | 992 | 1028 |

*Factory-fitted optional extras* (May 1965):

| | | | |
|---|---|---|---|
| Heater (Standard saloons)*: | £17 | 10 | 5 |
| Bench seat, facia-located parking brake and column gear change (De Luxe models only)**: | £12 | 1 | 8 |
| 1498 cc engine (Standard and De Luxe models)*: | £36 | 5 | 0 |
| Automatic transmission (all 1498 cc models, except G.T.)***: | £82 | 3 | 4 |
| Windscreen washers (Standard saloons)* | £2 | 8 | 4 |
| Wood-rimmed steering wheel: | £8 | 3 | 2 |
| Two-tone paint (De Luxe saloons): | £6 | 0 | 10 |
| Cloth upholstery instead of PVC (De Luxe and G.T. models)****: | £6 | 0 | 10 |
| Bright-metal side mouldings with or without two-tone paint (De Luxe Estate Car): | £8 | 9 | 2 |

    * Standard equipment on all other models.
  ** No extra cost on Super models.
 *** Bench or bucket seats optional at standard optional prices.
**** No price difference between cloth and PVC on Super models.

## INSTRUMENTS AND CONTROLS

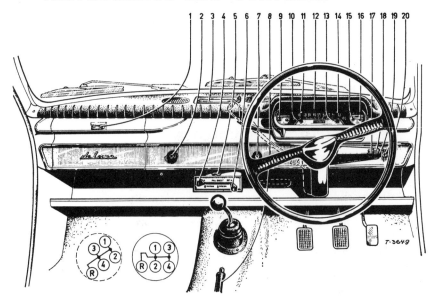

Fig. 8. Instruments and controls, r.h.d. (1963 model shown)

*Key to Fig. 8:*

1 Glove box
2 Choke control
3 Ashtray
4 Temperature control
5 Heater blower switch
6 Heater control, interior and screen
7 Windscreen-wiper switch
8 Parking brake lever (models with separate front seats)
9 Fuel gauge
10 Temperature warning light
11 Direction-indicator warning light, left
12 Speedometer
13 Oil pressure warning light
14 Direction-indicator warning light, right
15 Main beam warning light
16 Ignition warning light
17 Light switch
18 Direction-indicator switch
19 Horn button
20 Ignition and starter switch

# Dimensions and Weights

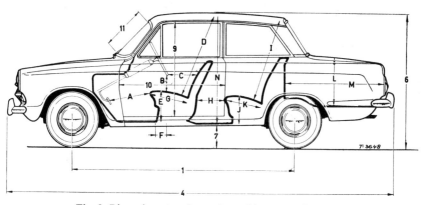

Fig. 9. Dimensions, two-door saloon with separate front seats

## EXTERIOR DIMENSIONS

|  | (inches) |
|---|---|
| 1 Wheelbase: | 98¼ |
| 2 Track, front: | 49½ |
| 3 Track, rear: | 49½ |
| 4 Overall length: | 170½ |
| 5 Overall width: | 63 |
| 6 Overall height: | 57 |
| 7 Ground clearance: | 6½ |
| 8 Turning circle: | 34 ft 3 in |
| 9 Height of door opening: | 37½ |
| 10 Width of door opening: | 40½ |
| 11 Height of windscreen: | 19 |

## INTERIOR DIMENSIONS (front seat in central position)

*(inches)*

| | | |
|---|---|---|
| A | Pedal to front seat: | 17¾ |
| B | Steering wheel to seat: | 5¾ |
| C | Steering wheel to seat back-rest: | 14½ |
| D | Height over front seat: | 37½ |
| E | Height of front seat: | 11½ |
| F | Maximum adjustment of front seat: | 4¼ |
| G | Depth of front seat: | 19¼ |
| H | Front seat back-rest to rear seat: | 12 |
| I | Height over rear seat: | 35½ |
| J | Height of rear seat: | 11¾ |
| K | Depth of rear seat: | 17 |
| L | Height of luggage compartment: | 18 |
| M | Depth of luggage compartment: | 42½ |
| N | Maximum interior height: | 46 |
| | Width of luggage compartment: | 53½ |
| | Height of tail-gate opening (Estate Car): | 30 |
| | Width of tail-gate opening (Estate Car): | 46½ |

## WEIGHTS (lbs)

| | dry weight | complete car ready for use | ratio of load on front and rear axles |
|---|---|---|---|
| 1200 – 2-door de Luxe: | 1720 | 1775 | 54/46 |
| 1200 – 4-door de Luxe: | 1748 | 1803 | |
| 1500 – 2-door Super: | 1808 | 1863 | |
| 1500 – 4-door Super: | 1844 | 1899 | 55·5/44·5 |
| 1200 – Estate Car: | 1928 | 1988 | 49/51 |
| 1500 – Estate Car: | 2024 | 2084 | |

# Technical Specifications

## ENGINE

| | 1200 | 1500 |
|---|---|---|
| Model: | 1200 | 1500 |
| Type: | four-stroke, petrol, water-cooled | |
| Cylinders: | four | |
| Valve arrangement: | overhead (pushrods) | |
| Bore and stroke (in): | 3·1875 × 2·29 | 3·1875 × 2·86 |
| (mm): | 80·96 × 58·17 | 80·96 × 72·75 |
| Cubic capacity (cu in): | 73·09 | 91·4 |
| (cc): | 1198 | 1498 |
| Compression ratio: | 8·7 : 1* | 8·3 : 1** |
| Maximum bhp at rpm (gross): | 53 at 4800 | |
| (net): | 48·5 at 4800 | 59·5 at 4600 |
| Maximum bmep at rpm (lb/sq in): | 178 | 183 |

*7·3:1 optional, 1965–66 models: 9·1:1, bhp 54 (gross) at 5000rpm
**7·0:1 optional, 1965–66 models: 9·0:1, bhp 65 (gross) at 4800rpm

| | | |
|---|---|---|
| Maximum torque at rpm (gross): | 66·5 at 2700* | 85·5 at 2700** |
| (lb ft) (net): | 63·5 at 2700 | 81·5 at 2300 |
| Mean piston speed at max. bhp (ft/min): | 1825 | 2200 |
| Top gear mph at 1000 rpm: | 16·1 | 17·3 |

*1965–66 models: 69 at 2700 rpm. **1965–66 models: 88·5 at 2500 rpm

## TRANSMISSION

| | |
|---|---|
| Clutch: | single dry plate; 7·25 in |
| Gearbox: | four-speed (all forward gears synchronized) |
| Gearbox ratios to 1: | 1·00 – 1·412 – 2·396 – 3·543; R. 3·963 |
| Final drive and ratio: | hypoid bevel |
| 1200: | 4·125 : 1 |
| 1500: | 3·9 : 1 |
| Estate Car: | 4·44 : 1 (Super and 1500 De Luxe: 3·9 or 4·1 : 1) |
| Overall gear ratios to 1, 1200: | 4·125 – 5·824 – 9·883 – 14·615; R. 16·347 |
| 1500: | 3·90 – 5·50 – 9·34 – 13·81; R. 15·45 |

## CHASSIS

| | |
|---|---|
| Tyre size: | 5·20—13 |
| | 5·60—13 (Super) |
| | 6·00—13 (Estate Car) |
| Brake lining area (sq in): | 81·68 (87 Super) |

(1965–66 models have 9½ in diameter disc brakes at front.)

## ELECTRICAL EQUIPMENT

| | |
|---|---|
| Electrical system: | 12 Volt |
| Battery: | 38 Ah (20-hour rate) (51 Ah optional) |
| Earthing: | positive |
| Ignition: | oil-filled coil |

## THEORETICAL ROAD SPEEDS (1200)

| rpm | first gear (mph) | second gear (mph) | third gear (mph) | top gear (mph) | piston speed (ft/min) |
|---|---|---|---|---|---|
| (a) 1000 | 4·5 | 6·5 | 11·5 | 16·0 | 380 |
| (b) 2700 | 12·0 | 18·0 | 31·0 | 43·5 | 1025 |
| (c) 4800 | 21·5 | 32·0 | 55·0 | 77·5 | 1825 |

(b)=rpm at maximum torque.
(c)=rpm at maximum power.

## PERFORMANCE FIGURES:

NOTE: These figures are approximate and should be considered to be fair averages.

| | de Luxe (1200) | Super (1500) |
|---|---|---|
| Maximum speed (mph): | 76 | 83 |
| Cruising speed (mph): | 65 | 75 |
| Cruising range (miles): | 295 | 285 |
| Maximum speed in gears (mph), first: | 27 | 29 |
| second | 41 | 43 |
| third: | 69 | 71 |
| Fuel consumption (mpg): | 25–37 | 25–36 |

# Lubrication and Maintenance

**Running-in:** Do not exceed the following speeds during the first 500 miles: 45 mph in top gear; 30 mph in third gear; 20 mph in second gear; 10 mph in first gear.

Do not maintain these maximum speeds for long periods, but vary your speed occasionally and completely release the accelerator from time to time; avoid long periods of idling, full-throttle acceleration, and over-revving of the engine.

Change down to a lower gear when necessary: the engine must operate at normal rpm.

## GENERAL DATA

Engine:

Sump capacity, 1200 (excluding filter): 4–5* Imp pints (4·8–6* US pints)
1500 (excluding filter): 6–6½* Imp pints (7·2–7·8* US pints)
extra for filter:    0·5 Imp pints (0·6 US pints)

Oil viscosity:    summer and winter:    SAE 20W
below 32°F (0°C):    SAE 10W

Oil dipstick: at the left-hand side of the engine, next to the generator.

Oil filler cap: on top of the valve rocker cover.

Oil drain plug: in the lowest part of the sump; change oil when the engine is warm.

**Oil filter** (full-flow type): The oil filter is mounted at the right-hand side of the cylinder block. Clean housing and renew element every 5000 miles. Refit the filter assembly using a new rubber sealing ring.

**Air-cleaner** (gauze type): Clean the element every 5000 miles (under normal conditions). Remove the screw on top and then the cover. Wash the element in petrol, allow to dry and dip the element in engine oil. Refit after draining surplus oil.

**Air-cleaner** (paper element): Renew element every 15,000 miles. In dusty areas it is necessary to clean the element at shorter intervals (for instance, at every 5000 miles). Unscrew the top cover centre screw, lift the top and carefully remove the element. Shake it clean and refit, using new sealing rings.

**Fan belt:** The correct tension should allow ½ in free movement when the belt is pushed and pulled, mid-way between the water pump and generator pulleys.

If necessary adjust the tension.

**Gearbox:** Capacity: 1·75 Imp pints (2·1 US pints).
Oil viscosity: EP gear oil, SAE 80 EP.
Check oil level every 5000 miles.
Oil filler and level plug: at the left-hand side of the gearbox.

**Automatic transmission** (Borg-Warner 35, if fitted):
Capacity (total): 11¼ Imp pints (13·5 US pints).
Lubricant: Automatic Transmission Fluid of approved type.
Fluid check: every 5000 miles, with transmission at operating temperature and engine idling, withdraw dipstick and wipe with a clean rag. Insert dipstick and again withdraw. If necessary, top-up to correct level.
Fluid change: periodic fluid changes are not required.

**Rear axle/differential:** Capacity: 2 Imp pints (2·4 US pints).
Oil viscosity: summer and winter, Hypoid oil SAE 90.
Oil level and filler plug: in the rear of the banjo housing.
No drain plug fitted.

*From approximately December 1964.

**Cooling system:** Capacity, 1200 (without heater): 9 Imp pints (10·8 US pints); 1500 (without heater): 10·75 Imp pints (12·9 US pints). Extra for heater: 1·5 Imp pints (1·8 US pints).

Drain taps: one in the radiator lower tank; one on the left-hand side of the cylinder block to the rear of the generator.

During frosty weather the cooling system must be protected by an approved anti-freeze solution.

Drain, flush and refill cooling system and check joints and hoses. At the same time check cylinder-head bolts for tightness. After filling with anti-freeze, check for leaks.

The water pump does not require periodic attention.

**Steering gear:** Capacity: 0·42 Imp pints (0·51 US pints).

Oil viscosity: EP gear oil, SAE 90 EP.

Check oil level every 5000 miles and if necessary fill up to the bottom of the filler plug hole.

**Front suspension units:** With car unladen and on level ground, remove filler/level plug. If necessary, top-up with special fluid (Ford Part No. M–1000502–E).

**Hydraulic brake and clutch fluid reservoirs:** These reservoirs are located on the scuttle in the engine compartment on the driver's side. Top-up with correct FoMoCo brake fluid. The level should be to the point indicated on the reservoir, approximately $\frac{5}{8}$ in from the rim. On models with plastic extension reservoir the correct level is indicated by a mark below the filler neck.

**Battery:** The battery is situated under the bonnet on the left-hand side. The positive terminal is earthed. Keep the terminals clean. When cleaning the terminals the filler plugs must be in place. Check battery electrolyte level; if necessary top-up with distilled water to approximately $\frac{1}{4}$ in above the separators. Never add acid.

**Front wheel bearings:** Every 5000 miles, adjust if necessary. Every 15,000 miles, dismantle, clean, repack with lithium-base grease, and adjust.

## TYRE PRESSURES

Check tyre pressures with an approved pressure gauge, when the tyres are cold.

|  | (lb/sq in) | |
| --- | --- | --- |
|  | front | rear |
| Saloon (1200): | 22 | 22 |
| Saloon (1500): | 22 | 24 |
| Estate Car: | 24 | 30 |

NOTE: Saloon with full load and for constant high-speed driving: front 24, rear 26.

# Routine Maintenance

*Daily:* Check oil level, radiator water level, tyres and lights.

*Weekly:* Check battery electrolyte, tyre pressures and fluid level of brake and clutch fluid reservoirs.

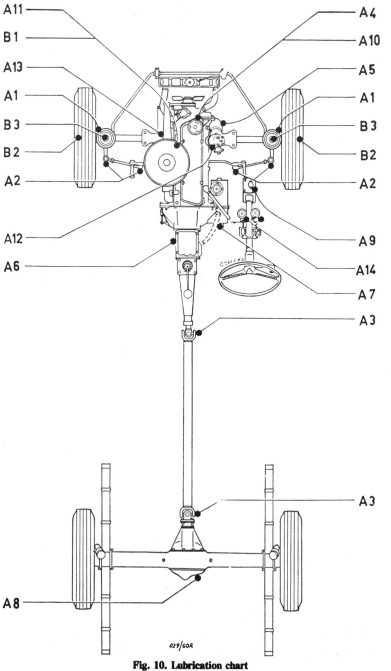

A11

B1

A13

A1

B3

B2

A2

A12

A6

A4

A10

A5

A1

B3

B2

A2

A9

A14

A7

A3

A3

A8

029/60R

**Fig. 10. Lubrication chart**

## A. Every 5000 miles:

*A1 to A3 incl.:* Lubricate with grease gun (no servicing required on models produced after September 1963).

*A*1 Track control arm ball-joints (2 nipples).

*A*2 Track-rod ball-joints (4 nipples).

*A*3 Propeller shaft universal joints (2 nipples).

*A*4 Engine sump: drain when hot and refill.

*A*5 Engine oil filter: clean casing, renew filter element, fit new sealing ring.

*A*6 Gearbox: check oil level, top-up if necessary. (After first 5000 miles only: drain when hot and refill.)

*A*7 Automatic transmission (if fitted): Check fluid level, top-up if necessary in accordance with the special instructions as outlined in 'General Data'.

*A*8 Rear axle/differential: check oil level, top-up if necessary.

*A*9 Steering box: check oil level, top-up if necessary.

*A*10 Crankcase ventilator: clean wire filter in petrol, dry and re-oil with engine oil; shake off surplus oil.

*A*11 Air-cleaner (wire gauze type): wash filter element in petrol, dry and re-oil with engine oil; shake off surplus oil.
Air-cleaner (dry type): if necessary, shake off dust from paper filter element.

*A*12 Ignition distributor: remove rotor and apply a few drops of engine oil on screw thus exposed, one drop on breaker-arm pivot and a few drops on automatic advance mechanism through gap round cam spindle. Lightly smear cam profile with grease or oil.

*A*13 Dynamo: lubricate rear bearing with a few drops of engine oil through oil hole.

*A*14 Brake and clutch fluid reservoirs: check fluid level, top-up if necessary.
Valve clearances: check and if necessary adjust.
Throttle linkage trunnion, parking brake relay lever (models with steering column gear change), locks, hinges, etc.: lubricate with engine oil.
Clutch: check free-play at operating cylinder.
Rear spring U-bolts: check for security.
Ignition distributor: clean and if necessary adjust contact breaker points gap.
Carburetter: adjust slow running.
Fuel pump: clean sediment bowl and filter.
Fan-belt tension: check, adjust if necessary.
Spark plugs: clean, adjust electrode gap if necessary.
Front and rear brake linings: check, road test and adjust if necessary.
Front wheel bearings: adjust.

## B. Every 15,000 miles:

*B*1 Air-cleaner (dry type): renew paper element, fit new sealing rings.

*B*2 Front wheel bearings: dismantle, clean and repack with grease, adjust bearings and fit new split-pin (do not entirely fill hubs with grease).

*B*3 Front suspension units: check fluid level, top-up if necessary with the car unladen and on level ground.
Front wheel alignment: check toe-in, adjust if necessary.

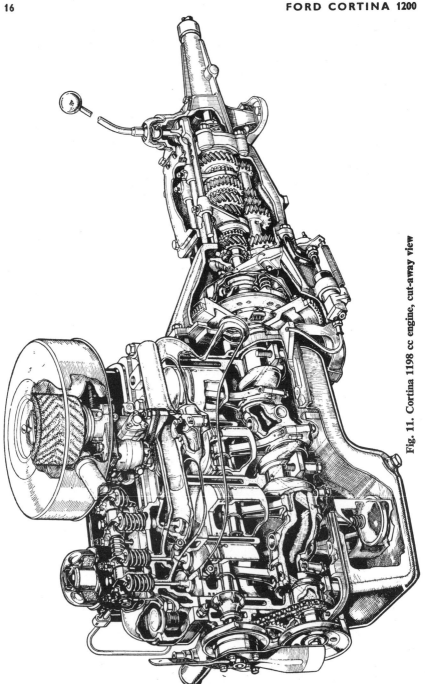

Fig. 11. Cortina 1198 cc engine, cut-away view

# Repair Data

Repairs are best performed by authorized Ford dealers, who possess the special tools and experience. The photographs used in this manual were supplied through the kind co-operation of the Ford Motor Company Ltd.

## ENGINE (1198cc)

NOTE: For 1498cc engine, see page 27.

**Engine type:** Water-cooled, four-cylinder, four-stroke, ohv engine. The engine forms a unit with clutch and gearbox, suspended in three rubber mountings.

*Removal and installation:*
Remove the bonnet after marking the hinges to facilitate reinstallation.
  Disconnect the battery.
  Drain oil and water. Jack-up the front of the car and place on stands.
  Remove the radiator hoses and the radiator.
  Disconnect the fuel pipe from the fuel pump and remove the breather pipe by removing one engine-to-bell-housing bolt.
  Remove the upper starter motor bolt.
  Remove the numbers 2 and 3 spark plugs.
  Disconnect the leads necessary to remove the engine.
  Disconnect the heater hoses.
  Remove the distributor cap.
  Remove the air-cleaner.
  Remove the exhaust pipe clamp bolts and disconnect the exhaust pipe from the manifold.
  Remove the second and fourth cylinder-head bolts on the left-hand side.
  Locate the bracket ends of the lifting bracket (tool No. P.6115A).
  Remove the engine splash shield.
  Remove the lower starter motor bolt.
  Support the gearbox. Remove the remaining engine bolts and the bolts securing the engine mountings to the cross-member.
  Pull the engine forward off the main drive gear and lift out the engine.
  Reinstallation is a reversal of the removal procedure.

**Engine compression:** The compression pressure at cranking speed with warm engine and wide-open throttle should be 175 lb/sq in (on engines with $8 \cdot 3 : 1$ compression ratio). Maximum permissible difference between four cylinders: 10 lb/sq in.

**Cylinder head:** Cast-iron cylinder head with integral valve seats and valve guides. When fitting the cylinder head, tighten the cylinder-head bolts gradually in the order given below to 65–70ft lb.

$$
\begin{array}{cccccc}
 & 8 & 6 & 2 & 4 & 9 \\
\text{front} & \rule{4cm}{0.4pt} \\
 & 10 & 3 & 1 & 5 & 7
\end{array}
$$

**Cylinder-head gasket:** The cylinder-head gasket should be installed with the steel face downwards: screw the locating stud bolts (P.T. 4063) into diagonally opposite bolt holes in the cylinder block face in order to locate the cylinder-head gasket and cylinder head.

**Cylinder block:** The cylinder block is made of cast-iron and incorporates the upper half of the crankcase. When measuring cylinder bores, this should be done at a point $1 \cdot 56$in from the top face of the cylinder block across the axis of the crankshaft.

Grade numbers are stamped according to the sizes of the pistons (see also under *Pistons*). When the cylinders are rebored during an overhaul, it is most important that each cylinder bore is machined to suit the individual piston to give the correct piston clearance.

**Inlet and exhaust manifolds:** The inlet and exhaust manifolds are bolted together to form a 'hot-spot' for pre-heating of the mixture.

**Engine sump:** The removable engine sump is a steel pressing. In order to remove the sump, remove the sump shield (if fitted), the engine splash shield and the starter motor. Take the weight of the engine in a tackle, remove bolts and nuts securing the mounting brackets and then raise the front of the engine 2 in.

Remove the bolts securing the sump to the cylinder block.

**Crankcase ventilation:** The air for crankcase ventilation enters the engine *via* a steel wool filter in the oil filler cap. The outlet is fitted to the right-hand side of the crankcase, on top of the fuel-pump boss.

**Pistons:** Light alloy, solid skirt pistons of the autothermic type, with two compression rings and one oil control ring above the piston pin. Pistons are available in standard size and 0·0025 in, 0·005 in, 0·015 in and 0·030 in oversize.

Each piston is marked with a grade number, which is stamped on the piston crown. This grade number should correspond to the grade number of the cylinder in which the piston is to be fitted. Piston clearance is measured by inserting the piston, together with a 0·0015 × 0·5 in feeler blade into the cylinder; a pull of 3–7 lb should be required to remove the feeler blade. The piston clearance should be measured at right-angles to the piston pin bore.

| *Piston grades* | *Standard bore* | 0·030 *in oversize* |
|---|---|---|
| Grade 1 | 3·1858–3·1861 in | 3·2158–3·2161 in |
| 2 | 3·1861–3·1864 in | 3·2161–3·2164 in |
| 3 | 3·1864–3·1867 in | 3·2164–3·2167 in |
| 4 | 3·1867–3·1870 in | 3·2167–3·2170 in |
| 5 | 3·1870–3·1873 in | 3·2170–3·2173 in |
| 6 | 3·1873–3·1876 in | 3·2173–3·2176 in |

Grades 5 and 6 are supplied for service use only.

When fitting pistons to connecting rods, the arrow on the piston crown should coincide with the 'front' mark on the connecting rod; heat the piston in oil or water prior to fitting the piston pin. Install the piston and connecting-rod assembly in the engine with the arrow on the piston crown pointing toward the front of the cylinder block.

*Specifications:*

| | |
|---|---|
| Width of piston-ring grooves: | |
| compression rings: | 0·0796–0·0806 in |
| oil control ring: | 0·1578–0·1588 in |
| Piston pin, offset: | 0·040 in |
| bore: | 0·8121–0·8124 in |
| diameter: | 0·8120–0·8123 in |
| Piston pin to piston clearance: | 0·000–0·0002 in (selective fit) |

**Piston rings:** Each piston is equipped with two compression rings and one oil control ring, which are positioned above the piston pin.

*Specifications:*

| | |
|---|---|
| Width, compression rings: | 0·077–0·078 in |
| oil control ring: | 0·155–0·156 in |
| Ring to groove clearance, compression: | 0·0016–0·0036 in |
| oil control: | 0·0018–0·0038 in |
| Ring gap: | 0·009–0·014 in |
| Ring to wall pressure, top compression: | 6·22–9·04 lb |
| lower compression: | 5·6–8·8 lb |
| oil control: | 5·35–6·90 lb |

When installing the piston rings, the word 'Top' on the compression rings should be facing upwards.

The top compression ring is chromium-plated, the second compression ring is stepped; this step must face the piston skirt. The ring gaps should be spaced at 120°.

**Piston pins** (gudgeon pins): Hollow steel, fully floating piston pins, retained in the piston by means of circlips.

**Connecting rod and connecting-rod bearings:** The connecting rods are steel forgings of the 'H'-beam section with sintered copper/lead or lead/bronze, steel-backed bearing shells with 0·001 in lead overlay. A steel-backed bronze piston-pin bush is pressed into the connecting rod.

*Specifications:*

| | |
|---|---|
| Connecting-rod length, centre to centre: | 4·419–4·421 in |
| Big-end bore (in connecting rod): | 2·0830–2·0825 in |
| Big-end bearing inside diameter: | 1·9380–1·9392 in |
| Crankpin to bearing clearance: | 0·0005–0·0022 in |
| Effective bearing length: | 0·83–0·87 in |
| Small-end bush inside diameter: | 0·8122–0·8125 in |
| Piston pin to small-end clearance: | 0·0001–0·0003 in |
| End-float on crankpin: | 0·004–0·010 in |

The connecting rods, bearing inserts and bearing caps should on no account be filed or scraped and no hand-fitting is permissible.

Tighten the connecting-rod bearing bolts to 20–25 ft lb.

**Crankshaft:** The crankshaft runs in three main bearings, equipped with thin-wall, steel-backed bearing shells with white-metal lining. The crankshaft end-float is taken by semi-circular thrust washers which are fitted at either side of the centre main bearing. The thrust washers should be fitted with the oil grooves facing the crankshaft flange.

The centre main bearing cap is provided with a 30° chamfer 0·03–0·04 in wide, between the bearing locating notch and the rear face of the bearing cap. Oil is fed into the groove formed by this chamfer through a 'V'-notch 0·07 in deep in the oilway at the locating tab-end of the bearing shell.

*Specifications:*

| | |
|---|---|
| Crankpin journal length: | 1·062–1·066 in |
| Main journal length, front: | 1·219–1·239 in |
| centre: | 1·247–1·249 in |
| rear: | 1·358–1·368 in |

| | |
|---|---|
| Crankpin journal diameter: | 1·9370–1·9375 in |
| Main bearing journal diameter: | 2·1255–2·1260 in |
| Regrind diameters: | 0·010, 0·020 and 0·030 in |
| Crankshaft end-float: | 0·003–0·011 in |
| End-float thrust washer thickness: | 0·091–0·093 in |
| Overall length: | 19·505 in |

**Main bearings:** The main bearings are white-metal, steel-backed shells. The main-bearing caps are provided with cast arrows, which should point to the front of the engine.

Before removing the bearing caps, mark them to ensure refitting in the original position. When fitting the two halves of the rear main-bearing oil-seal, coat them with graphite paste; never install this oil-seal dry or the main-bearing journal may be scored.

*Specifications:*

| | |
|---|---|
| Block bore for bearing shells: | 2·2710–2·2715 in |
| Main bearing shell wall thickness: | 0·0719–0·0722 in |
| Main bearing clearance: | 0·0005–0·0022 in |
| Tightening torque for main-bearing cap bolts: | 55–60 ft lb |

**Flywheel:** The flywheel is fitted to the crankshaft by means of a locating sleeve, a dowel pin and four bolts.

*Specifications:*

| | |
|---|---|
| Number of teeth on starter ring gear: | 110 |
| Maximum run-out: | 0·006 in |
| Clutch pilot bearing, type: | sintered metal |
|       inside diameter: | 0·6713–0·6725 in |
|       outside diameter: | 1·5743–1·5753 in |
|       length: | 0·495–0·505 in |

**Starter ring gear:** Starter ring gear of special alloy steel, shrunk on to the flywheel. If a new starter ring is fitted, the chamfer must be towards the rear face of the flywheel.

**Camshaft:** The cast-iron camshaft is positioned in the right-hand side of the engine crankcase and runs in three steel-backed, babbit-faced bearing bushes. The end-play is taken by a thrust flange which is fitted between the front of the cylinder block and a collar on the camshaft front end. The camshaft sprocket is fitted to the camshaft by means of a dowel pin and two bolts.

*Specifications:*

| | |
|---|---|
| Camshaft journal diameter: | 1·5600–1·5605 in |
| Bearing, inside diameter: | 1·5615–1·5620 in |
| Bearing length, front: | 0·75 in |
|       centre: | 0·64 in |
|       rear: | 0·75 in |
| Bearing clearance: | 0·001–0·002 in |
| End-float: | 0·002–0·007 in |
| Thrust plate thickness: | 0·176–0·178 in |
| Maximum cam lift, inlet: | 0·2108 in |
|       exhaust: | 0·2176 in |
| Cam heel-to-toe dimension, inlet: | 0·77082 in |
|       exhaust: | 0·76762 in |

**Camshaft drive:** Camshaft drive is by means of a single-row roller chain; a cam-and-spring-operated timing chain tensioner is fitted.
Number of teeth on crankshaft sprocket: 17
Number of teeth on camshaft sprocket: 34
When fitting the sprockets and chain, the marked teeth on both sprockets should be on the centre-line facing each other.

**Valve timing:** The valve timing should be checked with $0 \cdot 015$ in inlet and $0 \cdot 027$ in exhaust valve clearance on a cold engine.

Inlet valve opens: 17° B.T.D.C.
Inlet valve closes: 51° A.B.D.C.
Exhaust valve opens: 51° B.B.D.C.
Exhaust valve closes: 17° A.T.D.C.

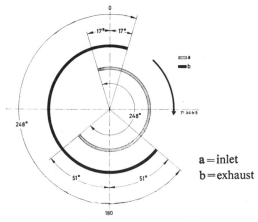

a = inlet
b = exhaust

**Fig. 12. Timing diagram**

**Valve clearance:**
Valve clearance, working temperature: $0 \cdot 010$ in inlet
$0 \cdot 017$ in exhaust
Valve clearance, cold engine: $0 \cdot 008$ in inlet
$0 \cdot 018$ in exhaust

**Valves:** Overhead valves, push-rod operated. Valve material, inlet: En. 18D; exhaust, head: 21–4NS, stem: En. 18D.

*Specifications:*
Valve head, diameter, inlet: $1 \cdot 262$–$1 \cdot 272$ in
                      exhaust: $1 \cdot 183$–$1 \cdot 193$ in
Valve stem diameter, inlet: $0 \cdot 3095$–$0 \cdot 3105$ in
                      exhaust: $0 \cdot 3086$–$0 \cdot 3096$ in
Valve stem to guide clearance, inlet: $0 \cdot 0008$–$0 \cdot 003$ in
                      exhaust: $0 \cdot 0017$–$0 \cdot 0039$ in
Valve lift, inlet: $0 \cdot 315$ in
             exhaust: $0 \cdot 319$ in
Valve seat angle, inlet and exhaust: 45°
Valves with $0 \cdot 003$ and $0 \cdot 015$ in oversize stems are available.

**Valve springs:** Single valve springs.

| | |
|---|---|
| Free length: | 1·48 in |
| Spring pressure, fitted: | 46·5 lb |

**Valve guides:** Valve guides integral with cylinder head. Bore 0·3113–0·3125 in.
If necessary to fit new valves with oversize stem, the valve guide should be reamed to suit the valve stem.

**Valve seat inserts:** Valve seat inserts are available for both inlet and exhaust valves. Cut the recesses for the valve seat inserts to the dimensions given below. It is not necessary to freeze the inserts before fitting.

| Insert | Valve | Internal diameter in head | Depth of recess in head |
|---|---|---|---|
| Standard | inlet | 1·4195–1·4200 in | 0·2175–0·2225 in |
| | exhaust | 1·2680–1·2685 in | 0·2175–0·2225 in |
| 0·010 in oversize diameter, | inlet | 1·4295–1·4300 in | 0·2175–0·2225 in |
| standard depth | exhaust | 1·2780–1·2785 in | 0·2175–0·2225 in |
| 0·010 in oversize diameter | inlet | 1·4295–1·4300 in | 0·2275–0·2325 in |
| and depth | exhaust | 1·2780–1·2785 in | 0·2275–0·2325 in |
| 0·020 in oversize diameter | inlet | 1·4395–1·4400 in | 0·2175–0·2225 in |
| standard depth | exhaust | 1·2880–1·2885 in | 0·2175–0·2225 in |
| 0·020 in oversize diameter | inlet | 1·4395–1·4400 in | 0·2375–0·2425 in |
| and depth | exhaust | 1·2880–1·2885 in | 0·2375–0·2425 in |

**Valve tappets:** Valve tappets of the mushroom type. When removing the valve tappets from the cylinder block, be sure to note the location of each tappet in order that it may be reinstalled in its original bore.

**Valve rockers and rocker shaft:** The valve rockers are assembled on to the hollow steel rocker shaft, which rests in four supports on the cylinder head. The seat of the front rocker-shaft support on the cylinder head is provided with an oil hole. When the valve rockers and related parts are removed from the rocker shaft, they should be reassembled in the following order:

Fit a new split-pin in one end of the rocker shaft, install a flat steel washer, a spring cup washer and a second flat washer on the shaft; slide a rocker on the shaft, followed by a rocker-shaft support. (The bolt holes in the rocker-shaft support must be on the same side as the adjusting screw in the valve rockers.) Now install a rocker, a spring and a rocker, followed by a support, and complete the assembly in this manner. After the last rocker arm has been fitted, install a flat washer, the steel spring cup washer and another flat washer on the shaft; secure all parts in place by fitting a new split-pin.

**Lubrication:** Full-pressure lubrication by means of an eccentric bi-rotor or vane-type oil pump incorporated in the head of the full-flow oil filter, which is mounted at the right-hand side of the engine. The oil pump is driven by the camshaft by means of skew gears; the oil enters the pump through a filter screen which is fitted to the pump suction pipe in the oil sump.

Incorporated in the oil pump is a pressure relief valve which, when open, allows the oil to return to the sump. This oil returns via a pipe to the base of the sump, thus preventing aeration of the oil. Oil from the sump is fed to the full-flow filter which is fitted to the pump housing. From the oil filter, the oil is fed through a cross-drilling above the centre main bearing to the main oil channel on the left-hand side of the engine. Oil is also fed via a short gallery to the oil pressure transmitter unit on the right-hand side of the engine. Separate oil channels feed oil from the main oil gallery to each main bearing. The connecting-rod bearings are supplied with oil from the main bearings via drilled passages in the crankshaft. A small oil hole is incorporated in each connecting-rod shoulder which allows a jet of oil to lubricate the non-thrust side of the cylinders at each revolution of the crankshaft.

The camshaft bearings are fed via channels in the cylinder block from the three main bearings. A flat is machined on the front camshaft journal, allowing oil to be fed through channels in the cylinder block and head to the front rocker-shaft support, from where the oil enters the hollow rocker-shaft to lubricate the valve rockers. Each valve rocker is drilled for lubrication of the valve stems and push-rods.

The oil feed to the rocker-shaft assembly is at a reduced pressure, the system being pressurized once per revolution of the camshaft.

The timing gears and chain are lubricated by a constant supply of oil from a drilling between the crankshaft and camshaft front bearings.

**Oil pressure:** The normal oil pressure is 35–40 lb/sq in; the oil pressure warning light remains on as long as the pressure is less than 5–7 lb/sq in.

**Oil pressure relief valve:** The oil pressure relief valve is incorporated in the oil pump and is non-adjustable.

**Oil pump:** An oil pump of the vane or bi-rotor type is fitted at the right-hand side of the crankcase; the pump is driven by the camshaft.

The clearance between the lobes of the inner and outer rotors should not exceed 0·006 in; the clearance between the outer rotor and the pump housing should not exceed 0·010 in.

New rotors are available as a matched pair only. The end-clearance of the rotors should not exceed 0·005 in; if necessary, the face of the pump body can be lapped on a flat surface to obtain the correct rotor end-clearance.

The clearances mentioned above are suitable for both types of pumps.

**Oil filter:** Full-flow oil filter, positioned on the oil pump housing. When fitting the filter housing, always install a new sealing ring.

Do not fit the sealing ring at one point and work it around the groove, because the rubber will stretch and could cause an oil leak. Always fit the 'O' ring into the groove in the pump body starting at four diametrically opposite points.

**Ignition system:** Ignition by means of coil and battery. Firing order: 1–2–4–3 (number 1 cylinder nearest to the radiator).

**Ignition timing:** The contact breaker points should just start to open when the timing mark on the crankshaft pulley is in line with the pointer on the timing gear cover and No. 1 cylinder is at the end of the compression stroke.

To time the distributor, proceed as follows:

Install the distributor so that the rotor contact is in line with the low-tension terminal on the distributor housing and the vacuum control spindle is parallel to the engine.

Secure the distributor to the cylinder block with bolt and lock washer through the clamp plate.

Slacken the clamp plate bolt; take up any lost motion in the drive by turning the rotor clockwise as far as it will go and turn the distributor housing clockwise until the breaker contacts are just opening.

Tighten the clamp bolt. With the fourth line on the ignition timing scale (counting from the vacuum diaphragm housing) in line with the edge of the distributor body the timing is set at 6° B.T.D.C.

A slight readjustment to the distributor may be necessary to suit the particular type of fuel in use and the setting should be corrected after checking the timing as described above, or after road test. If necessary, correction can be made by means of the vernier control of the distributor housing.

**Distributor:** Distributor with centrifugal and vacuum advance.

| | |
|---|---|
| Breaker point gap: | 0·014–0·016in |
| Breaker arm spring tension: | 18–24oz |
| Condenser capacity: | 0·18–0·22 microfarad |
| Distributor shaft diameter: | 0·4895–0·490in |
| End-clearance: | 0·002–0·006in |
| Radial clearance: | 0·000–0·0015in |
| Automatic advance (no vacuum): | |
| Starts at: | 1·250rpm (crankshaft), 8·7 compression ratio |
| | 1·325rpm (crankshaft), 7·3 compression ratio |
| Ends at: | 5·000rpm (crankshaft), 8·7 compression ratio |
| | 5·000rpm (crankshaft), 7·3 compression ratio |
| Distributor identification number (on body): | 40857—high compression |
| | 40856—low compression |
| Colour of low tension terminal washer: | high compression: brown |
| | low compression: yellow |
| Identification numbers of vacuum advance unit: | 5, 17, 10—high compression |
| | 5, 16, 12—low compression |

*Centrifugal advance (distributor degrees at distributor rpm, on deceleration):*

| | *Degrees advance* high-*compression engine* | | *Degrees advance* low-*compression engine* |
|---|---|---|---|
| 2,800 rpm | 13½°–15½° | 2,800 rpm | 13½°–15½° |
| 2,500 | 13½°–15½° | 2,500 | 13½°–15½° |
| 2,150 | 12°–14° | 2,150 | 12°–14° |
| 1,600 | 9½°–11½° | 1,600 | 9½°–11½° |
| 1,100 | 7½°–9½° | 1,400 | 7½°–9½° |
| 900 | 5°–7° | 800 | ½°–2½° |
| 700 | 1°–3° | 650 | 0°–1° |
| 550 | no advance | 575 | no advance |

*Vacuum advance, distributor degrees:*

| *Low-compression engine* | *High-compression engine* |
|---|---|
| 0°–1° at 5in Hg | ¼°–2½° at 6in Hg |
| 1½°–4° at 6½in Hg | 3°–5° at 8in Hg |
| 6°–8° at 9½in Hg | 6½°–8½° at 11in Hg |
| 9¾°–11¾° at 13in Hg | 8°–10° at 13in Hg |
| 11°–13° at 20in Hg | 9°–11° at 20in Hg |

NOTE: The advance should only be measured on deceleration, i.e. with the distributor slowing down on the test unit.

**Spark plugs:** Champion, type N5, or Autolite AG32 (later production), 14mm.
Spark-plug gap: 0·023–0·028 in.

**Fuel system:** The fuel tank is situated under the floor of the luggage compartment.
The tank capacity is 8 Imp gallons (9·6 US gallons).
The fuel is fed to the downdraught carburettor by means of a mechanically-operated pump of the diaphragm type.
On high-compression engines only premium grade fuel should be used. High-compression engines can be identified by the letter 'H' stamped on an inlet manifold mounting pad.

**Carburettor:** Single-barrel downdraught carburettor, Solex B30 PSEI–2.
*Specifications:*

| | |
|---|---|
| Main jet: | 110 |
| Main air bleed: | 200 |
| Accelerator pump jet: | 40 |
| Idling air bleed: | 60 |
| Idling jet: | 50 |
| Economy jet: | 65 |
| Econostat air bleed: | 130 |
| Econostat jet: | 80 |
| Choke tube: | 23 mm |
| Needle valve: | 1·6 mm |

**Fuel pump:** Mechanically-operated fuel pump of the diaphragm type.
*Specifications:*

| | |
|---|---|
| Pump pressure: | 1–2 lb/sq in |
| Diaphragm spring, test length: | 0·468 in |
| test pressure: | $3\frac{1}{4}$–$3\frac{1}{2}$ lb |
| Rocker-arm spring, test length: | 0·44 in |
| test pressure: | $5/5\frac{1}{2}$ lb |

**Air-cleaner:** An air-cleaner of the 'oil-wetted' gauze type is fitted to cars for the home market; a paper element or dry gauze type to export cars.
For maintenance details see 'Lubrication and Maintenance'.

**Cooling system:** The pressurised water-cooling system is of the impeller-assisted thermosyphon type; the water pump is bolted to the front face of the cylinder block.
The cooling system is equipped with two draincocks; one at the lower tank and one at the left-hand side of the cylinder block.
A thermostat is located in the upper water outlet.
*Specifications:*

| | |
|---|---|
| Cooling system capacity, without heater: | 9 Imp pints |
| with heater: | $10\frac{1}{2}$ Imp pints |
| Radiator cap release pressure: | 7 lb/sq in |

**Thermostat:** The thermostat is located in the upper water outlet.
*Specifications:*

| | |
|---|---|
| Thermostat starts to open: | 180°–190° F |
| fully open: | 214° F |

**Water pump:** Impeller-type pump with double-row ball-bearing. The pump shaft cannot be separated from the ball-bearing; if necessary, the shaft and bearing should be replaced as an assembly.

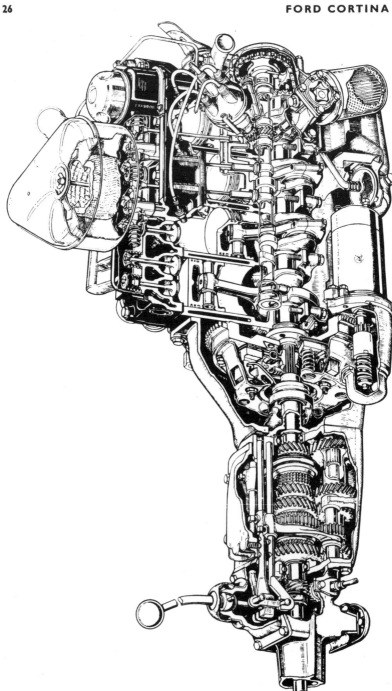

Fig. 13. Cortina 1498 cc engine, cut-away view

During pump overhaul, the impeller should be pressed on to the pump shaft until the clearance between the impeller blades and the rear face of the water-pump housing is 0·030 in.

**Fan:** Two-bladed fan; 11 in diameter.

**Fan belt:** Single V-belt, driving water pump and generator. The fan belt should be adjusted so that it may be flexed half an inch, measured between the water pump and generator pulley.

The tension of the fan belt is adjusted in the usual way by loosening the generator clamp bolts and moving the generator outwards.

## FORD CORTINA 1500
### **ENGINE** 1498 cc (optional equipment)

**Engine type:** Water-cooled, four-cylinder, in line ohv engine. The engine, clutch and gearbox are bolted together to form a single unit which is suspended in three rubber mountings. The crankshaft runs in five main bearings. The engine is available in two different compression ratios: 8·3 : 1 or 7 : 1.

*Removal of the engine:*
(1) Remove the bonnet, disconnecting the bonnet support at the lower end.
(2) Disconnect the battery.
(3) Drain oil and water.
(4) Jack-up the front of the car and place stands under it.
(5) Disconnect the radiator hoses and remove the radiator.
(6) Disconnect the handbrake cable from the handbrake relay lever.
(7) Disconnect the fuel pipe from the fuel pump; remove the engine breather pipe.
(8) Remove the upper starter motor bolt.
(9) Disconnect all wires necessary to remove the engine.
(10) Remove the distributor cap.
　　Remove the oil pump and filter.
　　Remove the heater hoses and the air-cleaner.
　　Remove the rocker cover. Remove the exhaust pipe clamp bolts and withdraw the exhaust pipe.
　　Disconnect the choke and throttle controls.
(11) Remove the second and fourth cylinder-head bolts on the left-hand side of the head. Locate tool No. P.6115A for lifting the engine out of the car.
(12) Remove the sump shield and the engine splash shield.
(13) Unscrew the lower starter motor bolt and remove the starter motor.
(14) Support the gearbox and remove the remaining bolts securing the engine to the clutch housing.
(15) Remove the engine mounting bolts, pull the engine forward off the main drive gear and lift the engine out of the car.

*Reinstallation:*
Reinstallation is carried out in the reverse order of removal.

**Engine compression:** The compression pressure at cranking speed on a warm engine with wide-open throttle should be 173 lb/sq in for high-compression engines and 144 lb/sq in for low-compression engines. The compression ratio is identified by an 'H' for the high-compression engines and an 'L' for the low-compression engines, stamped on top of the machined location pads above the valve ports.

**Cylinder head:** Cast-iron cylinder head, equipped with the valve mechanism.

B

Tighten the cylinder-head bolts evenly to 65/70 ft lb in the order given below:

```
7    5    1    3    10
─────────────────────── Front
9    4    2    6    8
```

Valve seats are machined directly into the cylinder head. When necessary, valve seat inserts are available. When fitting new valve seat inserts, a recess should be machined into the cylinder head. The sizes for the recess are given under *Specifications* for standard and oversize inserts.

*Specifications:*

Combustion chamber, depth:       0·580in (8·3:1 compression ratio)
                                     0·690in (7:1 compression ratio)

Combustion chamber, volume:     42·9–43·9cc (8·3:1 compression ratio)
                                     54–55cc (7:1 compression ratio)

| *Valve seat insert* | *Valve* | *Internal diameter of recess in head* | *Depth of recess in head* |
|---|---|---|---|
| Standard | inlet | 1·5620–1·5625in | 0·178 –0·180in |
| | exhaust | 1·2680–1·2685in | 0·2175–0·2225in |
| 0·010in oversize diameter, | inlet | 1·5720–1·5725in | 0·178–0·180in |
| standard depth | exhaust | 1·2780–1·2785in | 0·2175–0·2225in |
| 0·010in oversize diameter | inlet | 1·5720–1·5725in | 0·188 –0·190in |
| and depth | exhaust | 1·2780–1·2785in | 0·2275–0·2325in |
| 0·020in oversize diameter, | inlet | 1·5820–1·5825in | 0·178 –0·180in |
| standard depth | exhaust | 1·2880–1·2885in | 0·2175–0·2225in |
| 0·020in oversize diameter, | inlet | 1·5820–1·5825in | 0·198 –0·200in |
| and depth | exhaust | 1·2880–1·2885in | 0·2375–0·2425in |

**Cylinder-head gasket:** Steel cylinder-head gasket. Before fitting, both sides should be coated with sealing compound. In order to avoid damaging the gasket while fitting the cylinder head, the use of guide studs P.T. 4063 is recommended. Screw the guide studs diametrically in two opposite holes.

**Cylinder block:** Cast-iron cylinder block and crankcase.

*Specifications:*

| | |
|---|---|
| Bore: | 3·1875in |
| Cylinder bore standard sizes: Grade 1: | 3·1869–3·1872in |
| 2: | 3·1872–3·1875in |
| 3: | 3·1875–3·1878in |
| 4: | 3·1878–3·1881in |
| 5: | 3·1881–3·1884in |
| 6: | 3·1884–3·1887in |
| Cylinder liners available: | standard and 0·020 in oversize on outside diameter |

Bore for cylinder liners, standard:         3·3115–3·3125 in
         0·020 in oversize:            3·3315–3·3325 in
Camshaft bearing bore in block:        1·6885–1·6895 in
Main bearing bore in block:           2·2710–2·2715 in

The cylinder bores are graded; the grade letter is stamped on the camshaft side of the cylinder block. When fitting a new piston, the grade letter on the piston crown must be the same as the grade letter adjacent to the cylinder bore in which the piston is to be fitted.

The crankshaft main bearing bores are standard or 0·015 in oversize.

A cylinder block with 0·015 in oversize bearing bores is marked with a white paint dot.

The camshaft bearing bores are standard or 0·020 in; in the case of 0·020 in oversize, the cylinder block is unmarked.

**Inlet and exhaust manifold:** Inlet and exhaust manifold are bolted together to form a 'hot-spot'.

**Engine sump:** The removable engine sump is a steel pressing. In order to remove the sump, remove the radiator hoses, the engine splash shield and the starter motor. Loosen the front engine mountings and raise the front of the engine approximately 2 in.

**Crankcase ventilation:** The air for crankcase ventilation enters the engine via a steel wool filter in the oil filler cap. The outlet is fitted on the right-hand side of the crankcase, on top of the fuel-pump boss.

**Pistons:** Light alloy, solid skirt, cam-ground pistons, with thermal slots, are fitted. Each piston is equipped with two compression rings and one oil control ring above the piston pin.

Oversize pistons are available in standard and 0·0025, 0·005, 0·015 and 0·030 in oversize.

Each piston is marked with a grade number, which should correspond to the grade number of the cylinder in which the piston is to be fitted.

Piston clearance is measured at a point $\frac{3}{4}$ in from the bottom of the skirt at right-angles to the piston pin, by inserting a 0·0015 × 0·5 in feeler between the piston and the cylinder. A pull of 3–7 lb should be necessary to remove the feeler gauge.

If the cylinders are rebored, it is most important that each cylinder bore is machined to suit the individual piston in order to give the correct piston clearance.

*Specifications:*
Width of ring grooves, compression rings:     0·0796–0·0806 in
              oil control ring:         0·1578–0·1588 in
Piston-pin bore diameter:               graded
Grade—red:                        0·8121–0·8122 in
      yellow:                   0·8122–0·8123 in
      blue:                     0·8123–0·8124 in
Piston-pin bore offset:                0·040 in towards thrust side
Piston clearance in cylinder bore:      0·0008–0·0014 in
Piston grades: Grade 1:            3·1858–3·1861 in
             2:             3·1861–3·1864 in
             3:             3·1864–3·1867 in
             4:             3·1867–3·1870 in
             5:             3·1870–3·1873 in
             6:             3·1873–3·1876 in

Grades 5 and 6 are supplied for service only. When installing pistons to connecting rods, the arrow mark on the piston crown should coincide with the 'front' mark on the connecting rod; heat the piston in oil or water prior to fitting the piston pin.

Install the piston and connecting-rod assembly in the engine with the arrow mark on the piston crown toward the front of the cylinder block.

**Piston rings:** Each piston is equipped with two compression rings and one oil control ring, which are positioned above the piston pin.

*Specifications:*

Top compression ring:
| | |
|---|---|
| Material: | cast-iron and chromium-plated |
| Type: | tapered |
| Radial thickness: | 0·122–0·130 in |
| Width: | 0·077–0·078 in |
| Ring-to-groove clearance: | 0·0016–0·0036 in |
| Ring gap: | 0·009–0·014 in |

Second compression ring:
| | |
|---|---|
| Material: | cast-iron |
| Type: | stepped |
| Radial thickness: | 0·146–0·156 in |
| Width: | 0·077–0·078 in |
| Ring-to-groove clearance: | 0·0016–0·0036 in |
| Ring gap: | 0·009–0·014 in |

Oil control ring:
| | |
|---|---|
| Material: | cast-iron |
| Type: | 'Micro-land' scraper |
| Radial thickness: | 0·122–0·130 in |
| Width: | 0·155–0·156 in |
| Ring-to-groove clearance: | 0·0018–0·0038 in |
| Ring gap: | 0·009–0·014 in |

The top and second compression rings are marked 'Top' and should be fitted with this marking facing upwards.

**Piston pins** (gudgeon pins): Hollow steel, fully floating piston pins, retained in the pistons by means of circlips.

When fitting a piston pin to a piston, heat the piston in oil or water.

*Specifications:*
| | |
|---|---|
| Type: | fully floating |
| Material: | machined seamless steel tubing |
| Length: | 2·80–2·81 in |
| Diameter: | 0·8120–0·8123 in |
| Clearance in piston: | 0·000–0·0002 in |
| Clearance in small-end bush: | 0·0001–0·0003 in |

**Connecting rods and connecting-rod bearings:** The connecting rods are steel forgings of H-beam section with steel-backed bearing inserts lined with copper/lead or lead/bronze, with 0·001 in lead overlay.

A steel-backed bronze piston-pin bush is pressed into the connecting rod.

*Specifications:*
| | |
|---|---|
| Length between centres: | 4·799–4·801 in |

Big-end bore:                                    2·0825–2·0830 in
Bearing shell thickness:                         0·0719–0·07225 in
Crankpin to bearing clearance:                   0·0005–0·0022 in
End-float on crankpin:                           0·004–0·010 in
Effective bearing width:                         0·83–0·87 in
Small-end bush inside diameter:                  0·8122–0·8125 in
Undersize bearings available:                    0·002 in, 0·010 in, 0·020 in,
                                                 0·030 in and 0·040 in

Tighten the connecting-rod bolts to a torque of 20–25 ft lb.

The connecting-rod shoulders are drilled to form an oil squirt hole.

The connecting rods and caps are numbered to facilitate correct reassembly; the number is stamped on the camshaft side.

**Crankshaft:** The special cast alloy steel crankshaft runs in five main bearings with thin-wall, steel-backed bearing shells. The crankshaft end-float is taken by semi-circular thrust washers at the centre main bearing. The thrust washers should be fitted with the oil grooves facing the crankshaft flange.

*Specifications:*
Material:                                        special Ford cast alloy steel
Main bearing journal diameter:                   2·1255–2·1260 in
Main journal length, front:                      1·219–1·239 in
                     centre:                     1·247–1·249 in
                     rear:                       1·308–1·318 in
                     intermediate:               1·273–1·283 in
Main journal fillet radius:                      0·080–0·094 in
Main bearing shell thickness:                    0·0719–0·0722 in
Main bearing clearance:                          0·0005–0·0022 in
Block bore for bearing shells:                   2·2710–2·2715 in
Crankpin journal diameter:                       1·9370–1·9375 in
Crankpin journal length:                         1·062–1·066 in
Crankshaft end-float:                            0·003–0·011 in
End-float thrust washer thickness:               0·091–0·093 in
Crankshaft overall length:                       19·505 in
Undersize bearings available:                    0·010 in, 0·020 in and 0·030 in
Oversize bearings available:                     0·015 in outside diameter. Inside
                                                 diameter standard

Tighten the main bearing cap bolts to a torque of 55–60 ft lb.

**Flywheel:** The flywheel is bolted to the crankshaft flange by means of four bolts and is located by a locating sleeve and a dowel.

*Specifications:*
Maximum run-out:                                 0·006 in
Clutch pilot spigot bearing, type:               sintered metal
                          inside diameter:       0·6713–0·6725 in
                          outside diameter:      1·5743–1·5753 in
                          length:                0·495–0·505 in
Tightening torque, flywheel bolts:               45–50 ft lb

**Starter ring gear:** Starter ring gear of special alloy steel, shrunk on to the flywheel. Number of teeth: 110.

**Camshaft:** The special Ford alloy cast-iron camshaft runs in three bearings in the right-hand side of the engine. The bearings are steel-backed, babbit-lined bushes. The end-float is taken by a thrust plate, fitted between the front of the cylinder block and a collar on the camshaft front end. The camshaft sprocket is fitted to the camshaft by means of a dowel and two bolts.

*Specifications:*

| | |
|---|---|
| Journal diameter: | 1·5600–1·5605 in |
| Bearing inside diameter: | 1·5615–1·5620 in |
| Bearing length, front: | 0·75 in |
| centre: | 0·64 in |
| rear: | 0·75 in |
| Bearing clearance: | 0·001–0·002 in |
| Oversize bearing available: | 0·020 in outside diameter |
| Bearing bore in cylinder block: | 1·6885–1·6895 in |
| End-float: | 0·002–0·007 in |
| Thrust-plate thickness: | 0·176–0·178 in |
| Sprocket location: | offset dowel and two bolts |
| Maximum cam lift, inlet: | 0·2108 in |
| exhaust: | 0·2176 in |
| Cam heel-to-toe dimension, inlet: | 0·77082 in |
| exhaust: | 0·76762 in |

**Camshaft drive:** Camshaft drive is by means of a single-row roller chain with cam-and-spring-operated tensioner. Number of teeth on the crankshaft sprocket: 17. Number of teeth on the camshaft sprocket: 34.

When fitting the camshaft sprocket and chain, the marked teeth on both sprockets should be on the centre-line facing each other.

**Valve timing:** The valve timing should be checked with 0·015 in inlet valve clearance and 0·027 in exhaust valve clearance on cold engine. See also Fig. 12.

| | |
|---|---|
| Inlet valve opens: | 17° B.T.D.C. |
| Inlet valve closes: | 51° A.B.D.C. |
| Exhaust valve opens: | 51° B.B.D.C. |
| Exhaust valve closes: | 17° A.T.D.C. |
| Valve lift, inlet: | 0·315 in |
| exhaust: | 0·319 in |
| Valve clearance, warm engine—inlet: | 0·010 in |
| exhaust: | 0·017 in |
| Valve clearance, cold engine—inlet: | 0·008 in |
| exhaust: | 0·018 in |

**Valves:** Overhead valves, push-rod operated. The inlet valves have an aluminium-coated head; this aluminium coating serves to reduce the valve temperature. The inlet valves must not be ground or lapped, since this would destroy the thin aluminium layers.

*Specifications:*

| | |
|---|---|
| Valve head diameter, inlet: | 1·432–1·442 in |
| exhaust: | 1·183–1·193 in |
| Valve stem diameter, inlet: | 0·3095–0·3105 in |
| exhaust: | 0·3086–0·3096 in |
| Valve stem-to-guide clearance, inlet: | 0·0008–0·003 in |
| exhaust: | 0·0017–0·0039 in |

| | |
|---|---|
| Valves with oversize stems available: | 0·003 and 0·015 in |
| Valve face angle: | 45° inlet/exhaust |

**Valve seats:** The valve seats are cut integral in the cylinder head at an angle of 45°.

**Valve springs:** Single valve springs.

*Specifications:*

| | |
|---|---|
| Free length: | 1·48 in |
| Internal diameter: | 0·802–0·814 in |
| Total number of coils: | 6 |
| Wire diameter: | 0·151–0·153 in |
| Fitted length (valve closed): | 1·263 in |
| Spring load at fitted length: | 44–49 lb |
| Colour identification: | blue |

**Valve guides:** Valve guides are directly machined in the cylinder head. Worn guides may be reamed to an oversize of 0·015 in with tool No. P.6056–015. After reaming the valve guides, the valve seats must be re-cut to make sure that the seat is concentric with the valve stem bore.

*Specifications:*

| | |
|---|---|
| Bore for guide bushes: | 0·4383–0·4391 in |
| Valve guide inside diameter: | 0·3113–0·3125 in |

**Valve tappets:** Valve tappets of the mushroom type. When removing valve tappets from the cylinder block, be sure to note the location of each tappet in order that it may be reinstalled in the original bore.

*Specifications:*

| | |
|---|---|
| Tappet length: | 1·85 in |
| Tappet stem diameter: | 0·436–0·4365 in |
| Block bore for tappet: | 0·437–0·438 in |
| Tappet clearance in block: | 0·0005–0·002 in |

**Push-rods:**

| | |
|---|---|
| Push-rod diameter: | 0·250–0·254 in |
| Push-rod length: | 7·40–7·43 in |

**Valve rockers and rockershaft:** The valve rockers are assembled on to the hollow steel rockershaft, which rests in four supports on the cylinder head. The seat of the front rockershaft support is provided with an oil hole. If the valve rockers and related parts have been removed from the rockershaft, they should be reassembled in the following order:

Fit a new split-pin, followed by a flat washer, a spring cup washer and a second flat washer on the shaft; slide a rocker on the shaft followed by a shaft support. (The bolt hole in the rockershaft support must be on the same side as the adjusting screw in the valve rockers.) Now install a rocker, a spring and a rocker, followed by a support and complete the assembly in this manner. After the last rocker has been fitted, install a flat washer, a steel spring cup washer and another flat washer, and secure all parts in place by a split-pin.

*Specifications:*

| | |
|---|---|
| Shaft diameter: | 0·623–0·624 in |
| Rocker ratio: | 1·54:1 |
| Rocker bore: | 0·625–0·626 in |
| Shaft clearance in rocker: | 0·001–0·003 in |

**Lubrication:** Full-pressure lubrication by means of a bi-rotor type or sliding vane type oil pump which is situated at the right-hand side of the crankcase. The oil pump is driven by the camshaft; oil enters the pump through a filter screen which is fitted to the pump suction pipe in the oil sump.

Incorporated in the oil pump is a pressure relief valve, which, when open, allows the oil to return direct to the sump. This oil returns via a pipe to the base of the sump, thus preventing aeration of the oil. Oil from the pump is fed to the full-flow filter which is fitted to the pump housing.

From the oil filter, the oil is fed through a cross-drilling above the centre main bearing to the main oil channel on the left-hand side of the engine. Oil is also fed via a short gallery to the oil pressure switch on the right-hand side of the engine.

Separate oil channels feed oil from the main oil gallery to each main bearing; the connecting-rod bearings are supplied with oil from the main bearings via drilled passages in the crankshaft. A small hole is drilled in each connecting-rod shoulder which allows a jet of oil to lubricate the non-thrust side of the cylinders at each revolution of the crankshaft.

The camshaft bearings are fed via channels in the cylinder block from the front, centre and rear main bearing.

A flat is machined on the front camshaft journal, allowing oil to be fed through channels in the cylinder block and cylinder head to the front rockershaft support, from where the oil enters the hollow rockershaft to lubricate the valve rockers.

Each valve rocker is drilled for lubrication of the valve stems and valve push-rods.

The oil feed to the rockershaft assembly is at reduced pressure, the system being pressurised once per revolution of the camshaft.

The timing gears and chain are lubricated by a constant supply of oil from a drilling between the crankshaft and camshaft front bearings.

**Oil pressure:** The normal oil pressure is 35–40 lb/sq in; the oil pressure warning light remains on as long as the pressure is less than 5–7 lb/sq in.

**Oil pressure relief valve:** The oil pressure relief valve is incorporated in the oil pump and is non-adjustable.

**Oil pump:** The oil pump is of the bi-rotor type or the sliding vane type and is installed at the right-hand side of the crankcase; the pump is driven by the camshaft by means of skew gears.

*Specifications:*

| | |
|---|---|
| Capacity: | 2 Imp gallons/min at 2000 rev/min |
| Pump body bore diameter: | 0·500–0·501 in |
| Drive shaft diameter: | 0·498–0·4985 in |
| Drive shaft to body clearance: | 0·0015–0·003 in |
| Inner and outer rotor clearance: | 0·006 in ⎫ |
| Outer rotor and housing clearance, mfg: | 0·0055–0·0075 in ⎬ (rotor pump only) |
| wear limit: | 0·010 in ⎭ |
| Inner and outer rotor end-float: | 0·005 in maximum |
| Vane clearance in rotor: | 0·005 in maximum ⎱ (vane-type |
| Rotor and vane end-float: | 0·005 in maximum ⎰ pump only) |

**Oil filter:** Full-flow oil filter, mounted on the oil-pump housing. When refitting the filter housing, always fit a new filter sealing ring in the groove in the pump body at four diametrically opposite points. Do not fit the sealing ring at one point and work it around the groove, or the rubber will stretch, leaving a surplus which could cause an oil leak.

**Ignition system:** Ignition by means of coil and battery. Firing order: 1–2–4–3 (No. 1 cylinder nearest the radiator).

*Ignition timing:*
The contact-breaker points should just start to open when the timing mark on the crankshaft pulley is in line with the pointer on the timing-gear cover, and No. 1 piston is on the compression stroke. To time the distributor, proceed as follows:

Install the distributor so that the rotor contact is in line with the low-tension terminal on the distributor housing and the vacuum control spindle is parallel to the engine; secure the distributor to the cylinder block with bolt and lock washer through the clamp plate.

Slacken the clamp-plate bolt; take up any lost motion in the drive by turning the rotor clockwise as far as it will go and turn the distributor housing clockwise until the breaker contacts just open.

Tighten the clamp bolt.

The ignition is now timed to 6° B.T.D.C., using the lower timing mark on the timing cover.

Readjustment to the distributor may be necessary to suit the requirements of the individual engine and the kind of fuel in use. Correction can be made by means of the vernier control on the distributor housing.

**Distributor:** Two types of distributor are available, one for the high- and one for the low-compression engine. The distributors can be identified by the low-tension terminal; for the high-compression engines the washer on this terminal is brown, for the low-compression engines yellow. Identification numbers for distributors and vacuum advance units are the same as for the 1200 engines.

*Specifications:*

| | |
|---|---|
| Ignition advance: | centrifugal and vacuum controlled |
| Static advance (initial): | 8° before T.D.C. |
| Breaker-arm tension: | 18–24 oz |
| Condenser capacity: | 0·18–0·22 microfarad |
| Contact-breaker point gap: | 0·014–0·016 in |

*Distributor shaft:*

| | |
|---|---|
| Diameter: | 0·4895–0·490 in |
| End-float: | 0·002–0·006 in |
| Clearance: | 0·000–0·0015 in |

*Vacuum advance* (degrees distributor at in Hg):

| High compression | Low compression |
|---|---|
| 9°–11° at 20 in Hg | 11°–13° at 20 in Hg |
| 8°–10° at 13 in Hg | 9¾°–11¾° at 13 in Hg |
| 6¼°–8¼° at 11 in Hg | 6°–8° at 9½ in Hg |
| 3°–5° at 8 in Hg | 1½°–4° at 6½ in Hg |
| ¾°–2¼° at 6 in Hg | 0°–1° at 5 in Hg |
| No advance at 3 in Hg | No advance at 2½ in Hg |

*Centrifugal advance* (distributor degrees at distributor rpm) *on deceleration:*

| High compression | | Low compression | |
|---|---|---|---|
| | degrees advance | | degrees advance |
| rpm | distributor | rpm | distributor |
| 2500 | 12½°–14½° | 2500 | 14½°–16½° |

| *High compression*<br>*degrees advance* | | *Low compression*<br>*degrees advance* | |
| --- | --- | --- | --- |
| *rpm* | *distributor* | *rpm* | *distributor* |
| 2050 | 10½°–12½° | 2050 | 11½°–13½° |
| 1500 | 8°–10° | 1500 | 8°–10° |
| 950 | 5½°–7½° | 1100 | 3½°–5½° |
| 850 | 4½°–6½° | 800 | ½°–2½° |
| 700 | ½°–3° | 650 | 0°–1° |
| 600 | 0°–½° | | |

NOTE: The advance should only be measured on deceleration, i.e. with the distributor slowing down on the test unit.

**Spark plugs:**
Champion, type N5, or Autolite AG32 (later production) 14mm.
Spark-plug gap: 0·023–0·028mm.

**Carburettor:** Zenith single-barrel, downdraught carburettor.

*Specifications:*

| | |
| --- | --- |
| Main jet: | 92 |
| Compensating jet: | 112 |
| Compensating jet well air bleed: | 2·6 |
| Accelerator pump jet: | 50 |
| Idling jet: | 55 |
| Idling jet air bleed: | 70 |
| Choke tube diameter: | 29mm |
| Needle valve: | 1·75mm |
| Float level: | 21mm below top of bowl |

**Fuel pump:**
Mechanically-operated fuel pump of the diaphragm type.

| | |
| --- | --- |
| Pump pressure: | 1¼–2lb/sq in |
| Diaphragm spring, test length: | 0·468in |
|               test pressure: | 3¼–3½lb |
| Rocker-arm spring, test length: | 0·44in |
|               test pressure: | 5–5½lb |

## FORD CORTINA 1200 and 1500
## TRANSMISSION

**Clutch:** Single dry-plate clutch, hydraulically-operated. The clutch pedal operates the clutch master cylinder, which is mounted to the scuttle in the engine compartment.

The clutch fork is operated by the piston of the actuating cylinder, which is mounted on the clutch housing.

The reservoir of the clutch master cylinder should be filled to the correct level with hydraulic brake fluid.

The push-rod of the clutch actuating cylinder should be so adjusted that a clearance of 1/10in exists between the end of the push-rod and the clutch release fork.

The clutch pedal is of the pendant type and is mounted with the brake pedal in a bracket assembly which is bolted to the scuttle, beneath the instrument panel.

Bleeding the clutch control system is carried out in the same way as bleeding the hydraulic brake system.

*Specifications:*

| | |
|---|---|
| Clutch release fork free travel: | 1/10 in |
| Master cylinder, internal diameter: | 0·625 in |
| Actuating cylinder, internal diameter: | 0·75 in |
| Clutch disc lining, outside diameter: | 7·25 in |
| inside diameter: | 5·0 in |
| thickness: | 0·28 in |
| friction area: | 43·28 sq in |
| Pressure-plate diameter: | 7·38 in |
| Tightening torque for pressure-plate cover to flywheel bolts: | 12–15 ft lb |

NOTE: The clutch pilot bearing in the crankshaft can only be replaced after the flywheel is removed. Install the new pilot bearing with the flat face towards the crankshaft. When installing the clutch plate, the longer boss on the clutch-plate hub should face away from the flywheel. When installing the clutch pressure-plate assembly, make certain that the dowel pins are properly seated in the holes.

**Gearbox:** The Cortina 1962–65 may be equipped with either a floor-mounted or a steering-column mounted gear lever. From September 1965 only the former is fitted.

The gearbox is of the constant mesh type with four forward gears and one reverse; first, second, third and top gear are synchronized. The constant mesh gears are of the helical type.

*Dismantling:*

After the gearbox is removed from the car, it can be dismantled as follows:

Remove the clutch release bearing, the clutch fork and the clutch housing.

Remove the gear lever cover and the gearbox top cover, being careful not to lose the shifter-shaft lock springs.

Remove the shifter-shaft lock springs and balls; place all gears in the neutral position.

Unscrew the square-headed shifter-fork bolts after removing the locking wire.

Withdraw the third/top-gear shifter-fork shaft rearwards and lift out the sleeve fitted to the shaft.

Withdraw the first/second-gear shifter-fork shaft and remove the floating interlock pin. Rotate the shaft 90° and remove it from the gearbox.

Remove the reverse shifter-fork shaft to the rear, rotating it 90° clockwise to prevent it fouling the extension housing.

Lift the forks out of their grooves.

NOTE: Two interlock plungers are located in the forward face of the gearbox; take care not to lose them during repair operations.

Remove the speedometer driven gear and its bearing sleeve from the extension housing.

Remove the extension housing.

Mark the bearing retainer and the gearbox housing.

Using a brass drift, drive the countershaft towards the rear until its front end is free from the box.

Insert dummy countershaft (tool P.7113) and push the countershaft completely out of the gearbox.

The countershaft gear cluster will now lie on the bottom of the gearbox.

Remove the mainshaft to the rear. The top-gear synchronizer ring will be loose

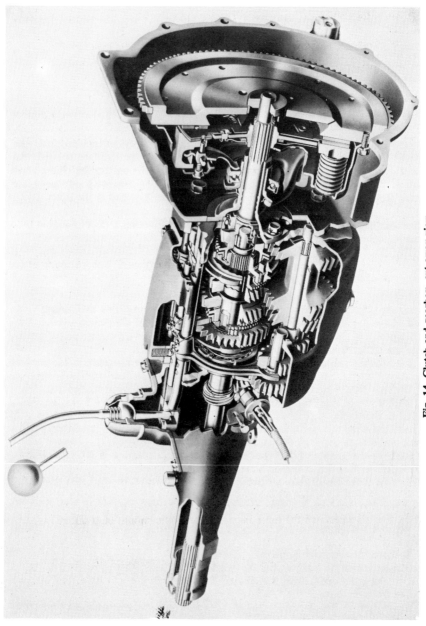

Fig. 14. Clutch and gearbox, cut-away view

on the main drive gear and may now be removed. Remove the thirteen rollers from inside the main drive gear.

Remove the main drive gear retaining plate and bearing retaining circlip. Carefully tap out the main drive gear.

Remove the countershaft gear with the thrust washers. The countershaft gear cluster is mounted on forty needle rollers (20 at either end).

Take care not to lose the needles and retaining washers.

With the aid of tool P.7043 withdraw the reverse idler shaft.

*Dismantling the mainshaft:*

NOTE: On the mainshaft is a machined collar which locates the second-gear pinion on one side and the third-gear pinion on the other. With special tools it is possible to remove the gears at one side of the thrust collar without disturbing the gears on the opposite side.

Tap back the tab of the tab washer and remove the nut of the speedometer drive gear. Remove the nut, tab washer and speedometer gear.

Remove the locating ball and spacer.

Remove the third/top-gear synchronizer assembly.

Remove the small circlip, place the mainshaft in a press and press the mainshaft out of the third/top-gear synchronizer and third gear.

Locate the adaptors around the front face of the second-gear pinion.

Press the mainshaft bearing, bearing retainer, first-gear pinion, first and second-gear synchronizer and second-gear pinion off the mainshaft.

**Important:**

The synchronizer hubs and sleeves are matched to each other and also to the mainshaft. Marks are etched on the corresponding splines of the hub and sleeve and near the hub and mainshaft splines.

The synchronizer and hub assemblies are serviced as a unit consisting of the synchronizer sleeve, three keys, two springs and the synchronizer hub.

The first-gear pinion runs on a steel bush, which is lubricated via three holes. Make sure that these holes are kept clear.

Remove the small circlip from the main drive gear and press the main drive gear out of the bearing.

Clean and inspect all parts thoroughly; renew those that are worn or damaged.

*Reassembling:*

Reassembling is done in the reverse order of dismantling. Take note of the following instructions.

Be sure that the marks on bearing retainer and housing and on mainshaft, synchronizer hubs and sleeves coincide.

Tighten the speedometer drive gear nut with a torque of 20–25 ft lb.

The clearance between the inner race and the circlip should be 0·002 in.

*Specifications:*

| | |
|---|---|
| Main drive gear, number of teeth: | 17 |
| internal diameter of gear end: | 0·9725–0·9732 in |
| mainshaft end pilot diameter: | 0·5960–0·5965 in |
| Countershaft gear, number of teeth: | $\begin{cases} 32 \\ 28 \\ 22 \\ 19 \text{ reverse} \\ 17 \end{cases}$ |

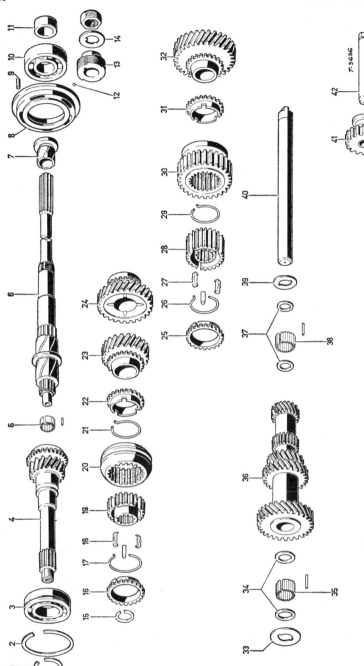

Fig. 15. Gearbox, exploded view

| | |
|---|---|
| Countershaft end-float: | 0·008–0·020in |
| Bore diameter for rollers: | 0·933–0·934in |
| Thrust washer, thickness: | 0·061–0·063in |
| Number of rollers: | 40 |
| Countershaft diameter: | 0·6818–0·6823in |

*First gear:*

| | |
|---|---|
| End-float: | 0·005–0·010in |
| Internal diameter: | 1·3763–1·3770in |
| Number of teeth: | 32 |

*First-gear bush:*

| | |
|---|---|
| Internal diameter: | 1·0495–1·0505in |
| External diameter: | 1·374–1·3745in |
| Finish: | phosphated |

*Second gear:*

| | |
|---|---|
| End-float: | 0·005–0·010in |
| Internal diameter: | 1·376–1·377in |
| Number of teeth: | 28 |

*Third gear:*

| | |
|---|---|
| End-float: | 0·005–0·016in |
| Internal diameter: | 1·376–1·377in |
| Number of teeth: | 21 |

*Reverse mainshaft gear:*
(First/second-gear synchronizer sleeve)

| | |
|---|---|
| Number of teeth: | 40 |

*Reverse idler gear:*

| | |
|---|---|
| Internal diameter: | 0·7500–0·7508in |
| Shaft diameter: | 0·7465–0·7470in |
| Number of teeth: | 22 |

*Speedometer drive gear:*

| | |
|---|---|
| Number of teeth: | 6 |
| End-float: | 0·000in |

*Key to Fig.* 15:

| | | |
|---|---|---|
| 1 Circlip | 15 Circlip | 30 Shifter sleeve |
| 2 Bearing circlip | 16 Synchronizer ring, top gear | 31 Synchronizer ring, |
| 3 Bearing | 17 Synchronizer spring | 1st gear |
| 4 Main drive gear | 18 Synchronizer keys | 32 First gear |
| 5 Needle rollers | 19 Synchronizer hub | 33 Front thrust washer |
| 6 Mainshaft | 20 Shifter sleeve | 34 Abutment rings |
| 7 Sleeve | 21 Synchronizer spring | 35 Needle rollers |
| 8 Bearing retainer | 22 Synchronizer ring, 3rd gear | 36 Gear cluster |
| 9 Dowel | 23 Third gear | 37 Abutment rings |
| 10 Ball-bearing | 24 Second gear | 38 Needle rollers |
| 11 Spacer | 25 Synchronizer ring, 2nd gear | 39 Thrust washer |
| 12 Locating ball | 26 Synchronizer spring | 40 Countershaft |
| 13 Speedometer drive | 27 Synchronizer keys | 41 Reverse idler gear |
| gear | 28 Synchronizer hub | 42 Reverse idler shaft |
| 14 Washer | 29 Synchronizer spring | |

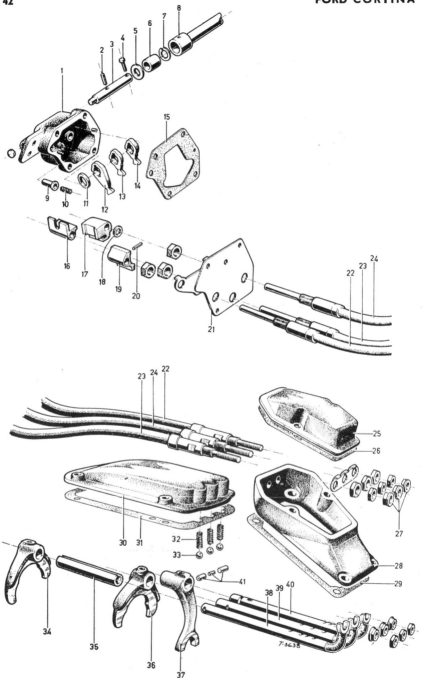

**Fig. 16. Shifter mechanism, steering column lever**

*Speedometer driven gear:*
Number of teeth:
standard (5·20—13) tyres—22
oversize (5·60—13) tyres—25

*Main drive gear snap rings:*

| Identifying colour | Thickness |
|---|---|
| Green | 0·0870–0·0899 in |
| Black | 0·0900–0·0929 in |
| Blue | 0·0930–0·0959 in |
| Orange | 0·0960–0·0989 in |

**Steering column gear lever:** The selection and engagement of gears with the steering column lever is obtained through cable linkage between the gate housing on the steering column and the cable abutment housing on the gearbox extension housing. The lower ends of the cables are threaded and equipped with collar nuts and locknuts, to provide adjustment of the cable length. When adjusting the cable length, use tool No. P.7115. The side cover of the gate housing is provided with a hole to fit this tool.

Run the collar nuts up the shaft over the full length and then back-off ½–1 flat. Secure the collar nuts with the locknuts. The total clearance at each cable should be 0·006–0·012 in.

**Propeller shaft:** Tubular propeller shaft with two universal joints. When removing the propeller shaft, mark the rear universal joint flange to ensure correct alignment on reinstallation.

**Rear axle/Differential:** Semi-floating rear axle with hypoid pinion and crownwheel.

**Rear axle shafts** (*removal and installation*): Remove wheel and brake drum; remove the four bearing retainer nuts, which are accessible via two holes in the

*Key to Fig. 16:*

1 Steering column shift housing
2 Selector pin
3 Selector housing shaft
4 Clevis pin
5 Washer
6 Bush
7 Circlip
8 Shifter tube
9 Reverse stop plunger
10 Reverse stop plunger spring
11 Thrust washer
12 Reverse selector lever
13 ⎫
14 ⎭ Forward selector levers
15 Gasket
16 Gate, 3rd/4th gear
17 Gate, 1st/2nd gear
18 Washer
19 Gate, reverse
20 Pin
21 Coverplate

22 Shifter cable, reverse
23 Shifter cable, 3rd/4th gear
24 Shifter cable, 1st/2nd gear
25 Cover
26 Gasket
27 Nuts
28 Cover extension housing
29 Gasket
30 Gearbox cover
31 Gasket
32 Detent springs
33 Detent balls
34 Shifter fork, 3rd/4th gear
35 Sleeve
36 Shifter fork, 1st/2nd gear
37 Shifter fork, reverse
38 Shifter fork shaft, 3rd/4th gear
39 Shifter fork shaft, 1st/2nd gear
40 Shifter fork shaft, reverse gear
41 Pins

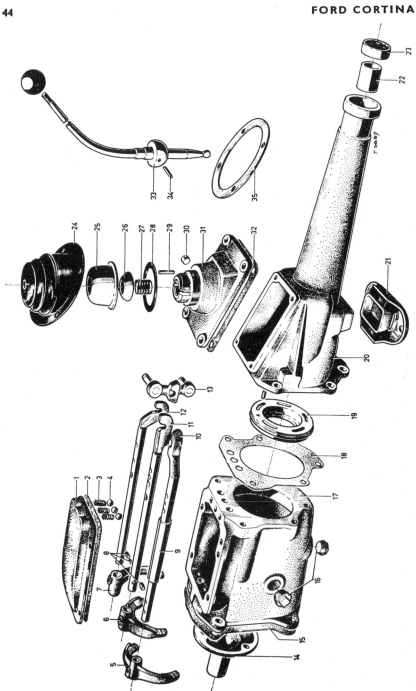

**Fig. 17. Shifter mechanism, floor lever**

axle-shaft flange. The rear axle shaft, together with the bearing and bearing retainer, may now be removed with the aid of a puller. If necessary, the axle-shaft bearing can be removed from the shaft with the aid of tool No. P.4090-6.

When a new bearing is pressed on to the shaft, a minimum pressure of 1200 lb should be required to do this; a pressure below this figure indicates an incorrect fit between shaft and bearing.

If a new axle-shaft oil-seal is to be installed in the axle-shaft housing, it should be driven in place with the aid of tool P.3072 and P.3072-3, making sure that the lip of the oil-seal is facing inwards.

**Differential** (*dismantling and reassembling*): Remove the rear wheels, the brake drums and the rear axle shafts; disconnect the propeller shaft from the pinion drive flange.

Unscrew the nuts securing the differential carrier assembly to the rear-axle housing and remove the complete differential carrier assembly. The differential assembly may now be dismantled as follows:

Unscrew the adjusting nut locking plate bolts and remove the locking plates.

Slacken the differential bearing cap bolts and back-off the differential bearing adjusting nuts with the aid of tool P.4079.

Remove the differential bearing caps, noting the markings on the bearing caps and differential carrier.

Remove the complete differential, together with the differential bearings and the adjusting nuts from the carrier; take care to keep the bearings and cups together to ensure that they are not interchanged when reinstalling.

Remove the stake lock on the pinion nut; unscrew the nut and remove the pinion drive flange.

Remove the pinion, together with the rear pinion bearing and the spacer bush, from the differential carrier.

Remove the pinion oil-seal, the front pinion bearing and the front and rear bearing outer races.

NOTE: Discard the spacer bush.

Remove the pinion rear bearing with the aid of tool P.4000-28 and a press; remove the spacer ring from the pinion shaft.

Unscrew the crownwheel bolts; support the crownwheel and press the differential housing out of the crownwheel.

Drive out the differential pinion shaft locking pin.

*Key to Fig.* 17:

| | | |
|---|---|---|
| 1 Gearbox top cover | 13 Reverse gear lever | 25 Cap |
| 2 Gasket | 14 Front bearing retainer | 26 Spring seat |
| 3 Detent springs | 15 Gasket | 27 Spring |
| 4 Detent balls | 16 Drain and filler plugs | 28 Seal |
| 5 Shifter fork, 3rd/4th gear | 17 Gearbox housing | 29 Retaining pin |
| 6 Shifter fork, 1st/2nd gear | 18 Gasket | 30 Breather |
| 7 Shifter fork, reverse | 19 Rear bearing retainer | 31 Cover |
| 8 Pins | 20 Extension | 32 Gasket |
| 9 Sleeve | 21 Mounting plate | 33 Shifter lever |
| 10 Shifter fork shaft, 1st/2nd gear | 22 Spacer | 34 Pin |
| 11 Shifter fork shaft, 3rd/4th gear | 23 Oil seal | 35 Seal ring |
| 12 Shifter fork shaft, reverse | 24 Dust boot | |

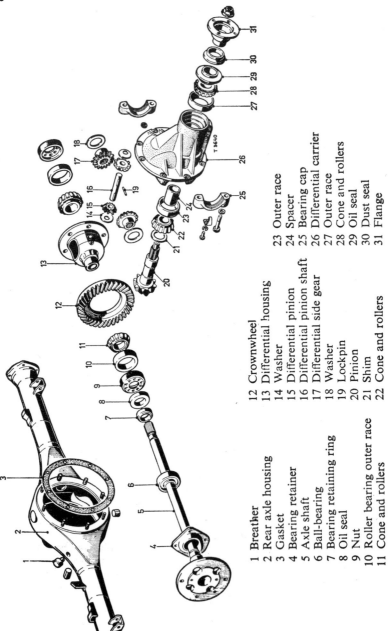

Fig. 18. Rear axle/differential, exploded view

1 Breather
2 Rear axle housing
3 Gasket
4 Bearing retainer
5 Axle shaft
6 Ball-bearing
7 Bearing retaining ring
8 Oil seal
9 Nut
10 Roller bearing outer race
11 Cone and rollers
12 Crownwheel
13 Differential housing
14 Washer
15 Differential pinion
16 Differential pinion shaft
17 Differential side gear
18 Washer
19 Lockpin
20 Pinion
21 Shim
22 Cone and rollers
23 Outer race
24 Spacer
25 Bearing cap
26 Differential carrier
27 Outer race
28 Cone and rollers
29 Oil seal
30 Dust seal
31 Flange

NOTE: This locking pin is tapered at one end and must be driven out from the crownwheel side of the differential housing.

Remove the differential pinion shaft, the differential pinions, differential gears and thrust washers.

If necessary, remove the differential bearings with the aid of tool P.4000–27 and a press.

*Reassembly and adjustment:*

In order to obtain correct adjustment of the pinion and crownwheel, the use of special equipment is essential; prior to assembly all parts should be oiled as usual.

Install the differential gears and differential pinions, together with their thrust washers; install the differential pinion shaft.

Fit the lock-pin by driving it into the differential housing from the right side, then lightly stake the differential housing to prevent the lock-pin from working loose.

Examine the mating surfaces of the crownwheel and differential housing for burrs; if necessary burrs can be removed by lapping with a fine stone.

Fit three suitable guide bolts in the differential housing flange; press the differential housing into the crownwheel with the aid of tool P.4080.

Remove the guide bolts and fit six *new* self-locking bolts, which must be tightened evenly to 30–35 ft lb.

Install the differential bearings with the aid of tool P.4086.

Install the outer bearing races of the rear pinion bearings with the aid of tool P. 4013–3.

*Pinion depth adjustment:*

Slide the rear pinion bearing over the dummy pinion P.4075–4; install the dummy pinion in the differential carrier and assemble the pinion front bearing and pinion drive flange.

Screw the bearing pre-load gauge adaptor nut on to the threaded end of the pinion.

Gradually tighten the flange retaining nut, at the same time turning the dummy pinion back and forth to ensure that the bearings will be properly seated.

Be careful that the dummy pinion flange does not foul the differential bearing cap supports.

Measure the bearing pre-load with the aid of tool P.4030; the bearing pre-load must be adjusted to 9–11 lb in.

If this pre-load is exceeded, loosen the drive flange retaining nut to remove all pre-load from the bearing and then gradually readjust the nut to give the correct pre-load.

The thickness of the pinion depth adjustment shim should now be determined with the aid of gauges P.4075 and P.4075–4. Set the gauge to zero by sliding the calibrating button across the machined underface of the gauge; set the dial to zero.

Clean the differential bearing supports and place the gauge in position so that the dial plunger rests on the face of the dummy pinion.

The gauge should be moved slightly backwards and forwards to ensure that the minimum reading is obtained.

If the pinion is marked with a plus figure, this figure should be added to the gauge reading; conversely, a minus figure on the pinion should be subtracted from the gauge reading.

Add 0·10in to the value thus found; this gives the correct thickness for the shims to be installed.

The following shims are available.

| | Thickness | | Thickness |
|---|---|---|---|
| 105E–4672–A: | 0·1304–0·1308 in | 105E–4672–H: | 0·1374–0·1378 in |
| 105E–4672–B: | 0·1314–0·1318 in | 105E–4672–J: | 0·1384–0·1388 in |
| 105E–4672–C: | 0·1324–0·1328 in | 105E–4672–K: | 0·1394–0·1398 in |
| 105E–4672–D: | 0·1334–0·1338 in | 105E–4672–L: | 0·1404–0·1408 in |
| 105E–4672–E: | 0·1344–0·1348 in | 105E–4672–M: | 0·1414–0·1418 in |
| 105E–4672–F: | 0·1354–0·1358 in | 105E–4672–N: | 0·1424–0·1428 in |
| 105E–4672–G: | 0·1364–0·1368 in | | |

Fit the correct shim on the pinion, with the internal chamfer on the shim towards the gear teeth. Fit the pinion rear bearing on the pinion with tool P.4000–28; fit the front pinion bearing in its outer race in the carrier. Fit the oil-seal in the differential carrier with the lip inwards.

Install the pinion with a new spacer bush in the carrier; fit the pinion drive flange and retaining nut and gradually tighten the nut until there remains a very slight end-clearance.

Locate the pre-load gauge adaptor (P.4030–1) on the pinion drive flange and fit the pre-load gauge.

Check the running torque required to rotate the assembly, allowing the pre-load gauge to drop through the horizontal position. This torque is caused by the resistance offered by the oil-seal to the drive flange, and when finally setting the pinion-bearing pre-load this figure must be added to the pre-load figure of 9–11 lb in for the pinion bearings alone.

For instance, if the torque required to rotate the drive flange is 5 lb in, the drive flange retaining nut must be tightened so that the assembly turns under a running torque of 14–16lb in. Gradually tighten the drive flange retaining nut, rotating the pinion to ensure that the bearing rollers are correctly seated until the required pinion-bearing pre-load is obtained. While making this adjustment, the pre-load must be checked frequently because, if the pre-load is exceeded, the assembly must be dismantled, the spacer bush removed and replaced by a new one.

When the correct pinion-bearing pre-load has been obtained, stake the drive flange retaining nut securely to the pinion with a suitable punch.

*Adjustment of tooth clearance:*
Install the differential assembly, with differential bearings and bearing outer races, in the carrier; fit the differential bearing caps and screw down the bearing cap bolts just finger-tight.

Refit the bearing retaining nuts.

Now install the bearing cap spread gauge (P.4009).

Fit one adjusting nut lockplate upside down on the left bearing cap, so that the plunger of the dial gauge rests against this lockplate. Set the dial of the cap spread gauge to zero and screw in the bearing adjusting nuts until a very slight end-clearance remains. Rotate the crownwheel during this operation to ensure that the differential bearings are correctly seated.

Install the tooth clearance gauge P.4008–1 in a hole on the differential carrier flange, allowing the gauge plunger to rest on the heel of a crownwheel tooth at right-angles to it. Adjust to zero clearance by means of the differential bearing adjusting nuts, then adjust the tooth clearance between the crownwheel and pinion to 0·001–0·002 in. The adjusting nut on the crownwheel side must be tightened last.

Swing the tooth clearance gauge out of position and, rotating the crownwheel all the time, screw in the bearing adjusting nut on the crownwheel side with tool P.4079, until a constant cap spread reading of between 0·005–0·007 in is obtained. Check this with tool P.4009.

Reposition the tooth clearance gauge on the crownwheel tooth and recheck the tooth clearance. Hold the pinion and rock the crownwheel backwards and forwards, noting the maximum and minimum readings on the gauge. The correct tooth clearance should be 0·005–0·007 in. If the tooth clearance is outside these limits, adjust the position of the crownwheel relative to the pinion by slackening the adjusting nut on one side and tightening the nut on the other side by a corresponding amount so that the cap spread is unaffected.

NOTE: The final tightening must be made from the crownwheel side.

Refit the adjusting nut lockplates (if necessary left- and right-hand offset lockplates are available). Tighten the lockplate retaining bolts to 12–15 ft lb.

Tighten the differential bearing cap bolts to 45–50 ft lb.

Check the tooth contact in the usual way by means of engineer's blue, red lead or yellow ochre.

Further assembly is done in the reverse order of dismantling.

If a new crownwheel and pinion have been installed, the axle should be filled with the special run-in lubricant, which is supplied with the new parts.

Check the oil level after 500 miles have been travelled and top-up with the specified lubricant (see *Lubrication and maintenance*), if necessary.

*Specifications:*

| | |
|---|---|
| Number of teeth on crownwheel: | 33 |
| Number of teeth on pinion: | 8 |
| Backlash: | 0·005–0·007 in |
| Pinion bearing pre-load: | 9–11 lb in (excl. oil seal) |
| Differential bearing pre-load (cap spread): | 0·005–0·007 in |
| Differential pinion thrust washer thickness: | 0·030–0·032 in |
| Differential pinion inside diameter: | 0·628–0·629 in |

## CHASSIS

**Chassis:** Body and chassis are welded together and form a single unit. For body and floor dimensions, see Fig. 19.

**Front suspension:** Independent front suspension.

The front suspension system utilises coil springs in conjunction with vertical-type shock-absorbers to form front suspension units. Each suspension unit is mounted between a ball-joint on the end of the track-rod control arm and a thrust bearing in a reinforced flange at the top of the engine compartment side wall. The upper mounting assembly allows the unit to rotate about its vertical axis to provide the necessary steering movement. The front wheel spindle, which carries the brake backing plate and hub assembly, is forged integrally with each suspension unit.

The inner end of each track control arm is mounted on rubber bushes in the front crossmember; the outer end is connected through a ball-joint to the steering arm.

A stabilizer bar is connected between the outer ends of each track control arm and is secured at the front to brackets mounted on the body side-members.

Each coil spring is located at the top in a seat on the suspension unit piston rod and at the bottom on a seat welded to the body of the suspension unit.

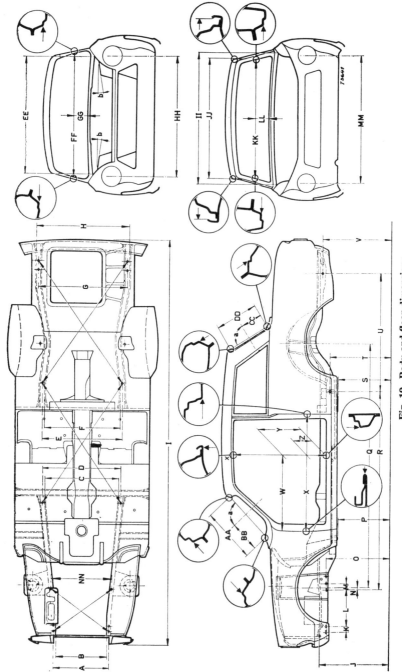

Fig. 19. Body and floor dimensions

Caster, camber and kingpin inclination are set in production and cannot be altered.

Each front suspension unit is provided with a filler plug; when topping-up, the car should be standing unladen on level ground.

On no account should shock-absorber fluid be added to the suspension units under pressure, or with a wheel jacked-up.

Whenever repairs are to be carried out on the front suspension system, it is essential that spring clips are fitted to the coil spring, otherwise extreme difficulty or personal injury may be experienced in dismantling and reassembling the parts.

NOTE: Wheel alignment should always be checked after carrying out repairs to the suspension unit or linkage.

*Dismantling:*

Fit spring clip P.5030 over as many coils of each spring as possible; connect the safety strap.

Jack-up the car and support the front crossmember on stands; remove the front wheels with brake drums and hubs.

Remove the brake backing plate after unscrewing the four self-locking nuts; provided the brake backing plate is suitably supported, it is not necessary to disconnect the brake hose.

Holding the suspension unit, remove the ball stud from the track control arm with a puller; also disconnect the track-rod ball-joint.

Open the bonnet and unscrew the three self-locking nuts securing the front suspension upper mountings.

Lower the suspension unit from the car.

Unscrew the self-locking nut retaining the upper thrust bearing with tool P.5025.

Remove the upper thrust bearing assembly, the upper mounting assembly and the lower thrust bearing assembly, being careful to avoid damage to the parts.

Remove the upper spring seat and the piston-rod shroud.

The coil spring (still held in the spring clips) can now be removed from the suspension unit.

Remove the filler plug from the outer housing and pump the fluid out of the unit by moving the piston rod up and down.

Carefully ease the stake lock from the slot in the piston-rod gland cap; now unscrew the piston-rod gland cap with tool P.5017–A.

*Key to Fig.* 19 (*inches*):

| | | | | | |
|---|---|---|---|---|---|
| A | 23 | O | 11 9/16 | CC | 8 31/64 |
| B | 21¼ | P | 7 9/32 | DD | 17¼ |
| C | 30 49/64 | Q | 98 (wheelbase) | EE | 48 9/64 |
| D | 31 61/64 | R | 78 61/64 – 79 3/16 | FF | 49 9/16 |
| E | 33 21/64 | S | 7 9/32 | GG | 11 11/32 |
| F | 31 35/64 | T | 9 7/16 | HH | 47 39/64 |
| G | 37⅞ | U | 45 13/16 – 45 15/16 | II | 51 23/64 |
| H | 39 39/64 – 39 43/64 | V | 13 17/64 – 13 29/64 | JJ | 47 7/32 |
| I | 159 15/16 | W | 22 7/32 | KK | 47 5/16 |
| J | 13 33/64 | X | 45 51/64 | LL | 8 31/64 |
| K | 2⅝ | Y | 20 1/16 | MM | 49 57/64 |
| L | 13 25/64 – 13 13/32 | Z | 10 1/16 | NN | 24 55/64 |
| M | 3 5/32 | AA | 20 25/32 | a | 90° |
| N | 35/64 | BB | 11 11/32 | b | 5° 36′ |

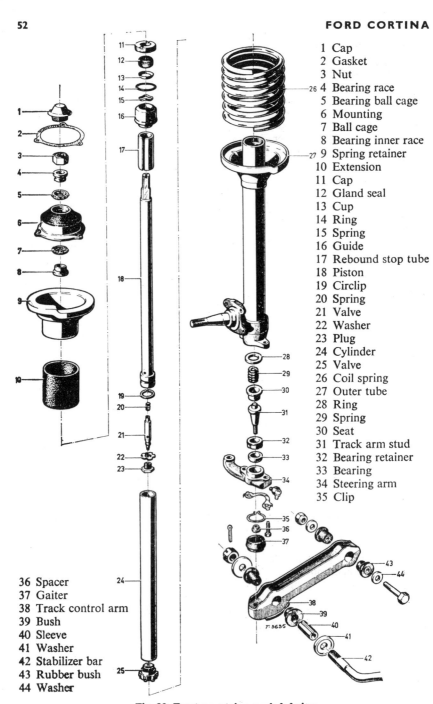

1 Cap
2 Gasket
3 Nut
4 Bearing race
5 Bearing ball cage
6 Mounting
7 Ball cage
8 Bearing inner race
9 Spring retainer
10 Extension
11 Cap
12 Gland seal
13 Cup
14 Ring
15 Spring
16 Guide
17 Rebound stop tube
18 Piston
19 Circlip
20 Spring
21 Valve
22 Washer
23 Plug
24 Cylinder
25 Valve
26 Coil spring
27 Outer tube
28 Ring
29 Spring
30 Seat
31 Track arm stud
32 Bearing retainer
33 Bearing
34 Steering arm
35 Clip

36 Spacer
37 Gaiter
38 Track control arm
39 Bush
40 Sleeve
41 Washer
42 Stabilizer bar
43 Rubber bush
44 Washer

Fig. 20. Front suspension, exploded view

Remove the rubber seal and pull the piston rod, the piston and cylinder out of the suspension unit.

Pull the valve assembly out of the base of the cylinder. The compression valve is incorporated in the hexagonal nut which projects from the assembly. In the end of this nut a small screw is situated which is adjusted in production. This adjustment should never be altered.

Remove the piston nut from the cylinder; the upper guide and the piston-rod gland will remain in the cylinder. Be careful not to lose the rubber gland or damage the upper guide when withdrawing the piston rod. Remove the valve unit from the piston-rod assembly after straightening the lock-washer tabs.

The adjustment of the piston valve is sealed during assembly and should not be altered.

Remove the piston-rod gland from the upper guide; lift out the gland cup and the valve spring from the upper guide.

Remove the upper guide from the cylinder.

The rebound stop tube can be removed from the top of the cylinder, although this is not normally necessary.

*Reassembly:*

Reassembly is done in the reverse order of dismantling, with attention to the following points:

The piston and piston rod are only serviced as an assembly, since these parts are machined after assembly in order to ensure correct alignment. The piston ring can be replaced.

If the rebound stop has been removed, it should be pushed into the cylinder until it is flush with the top of it.

Always install a new lock washer under the piston valve unit. One side of the gland is marked with the words 'This side down'; consequently, the gland should be positioned so that this side is towards the gland seat.

Always install a new seal ring in the suspension unit housing around the edge of the upper guide.

Tighten the piston-rod gland cap to 23–31 ft lb. using tool P.5017–A.

Stake the outer casing of the unit into the slot of the piston-rod gland cap.

After assembly, the front suspension unit should be filled with shock-absorber fluid as follows:

Place the unit vertically in a vice, with the piston rod in the lower position. Refill the unit with fluid through the filler plug hole, until it overflows. Move the piston rod at least six times up and down as far as it will go; then top-up with the piston rod at the lower position.

The thrust bearing locknut should be tightened to 45–55 ft lb.

Tighten the upper mounting nuts to 15–18 ft lb.

Tighten the brake backing-plate nuts to 15–18 ft lb.

After the front suspension unit has been reinstalled under the car, the front wheels have been fitted and the spring clips removed, recheck the fluid level in the suspension units and top-up if necessary.

*Specifications:*

| | |
|---|---|
| Caster: | 0°33′–2°3′ |
| Camber: | 0°40′–2°10′ |
| Kingpin inclination: | 4°26′–5°56′ |
| Toe-in: | $\frac{1}{16}$ in–$\frac{1}{8}$ in |

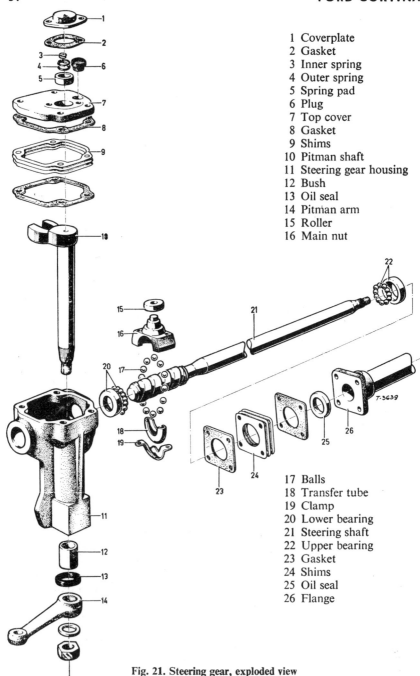

1  Coverplate
2  Gasket
3  Inner spring
4  Outer spring
5  Spring pad
6  Plug
7  Top cover
8  Gasket
9  Shims
10  Pitman shaft
11  Steering gear housing
12  Bush
13  Oil seal
14  Pitman arm
15  Roller
16  Main nut

17  Balls
18  Transfer tube
19  Clamp
20  Lower bearing
21  Steering shaft
22  Upper bearing
23  Gasket
24  Shims
25  Oil seal
26  Flange

Fig. 21. Steering gear, exploded view

| | | | 1963–66 |
|---|---|---|---|
| | 1963–64/1965–66 | | 1500 *Saloon* |
| Coil springs: | 1200 *Saloon* | *Estate* | & *Estate* |
| Spring length, free (in): | 12·25/12·40 | 12·40/12·25 | 12·40 |
| fitted (in): | 6·77 | 6·77 | 6·77 |
| Deflection rate (lb/in): | 91–99/100 | 96–104/95 | 96–104 |
| Number of coils: | 7·07–7·31/7·12 | 7·07–7·31/7·19 | 7·00–7·24 |
| Wire diameter (in): | 0·466–0·472/0·474 | 0·471–0·477/0·469 | 0·471–0·477 |
| Mean diameter of coils (in): | 5·46 | 5·46 | 5·46 |

*Toe-out (for 20° turn of outer wheel):* 1°8′–2°38′
Track: 49·5 in
Turning circle, between walls: 35·5 ft
between kerbs: 34·67 ft

| *Tightening torques* | *(ft lb)* |
|---|---|
| Stabilizer bar attachment clamp bush: | 15–18 |
| Stabilizer bar to front track control arm nut: | 25–30 |
| Front suspension thrust bearing retaining nut: | 45–55 |
| Front suspension unit upper support: | 15–18 |
| Front track control arm ball-stud: | 30–35 |
| Front track control arm inner bush: | 22–27 |
| Front wheel spindle nut: | 30 |
| Front brake backing plate to suspension unit: | 18–22 |
| Steering arm to front suspension unit: | 30–35 |
| Steering and idler arm joints: | 18–22 |
| Pitman arm nut: | 60–70 |

**Rear suspension:** Semi-elliptic rear springs; the front of each spring is secured to a hanger bracket welded to the body side-member, whilst the rear end of each spring is supported on a shackle.

When installing the rear springs, care should be taken to fit the spring U-bolts in the correct position.

The inner U-bolt has a notch on the inner radius which must be positioned towards the front.

U-bolt nuts must be tightened to 20–25 ft lb.

| *Spring specifications:* | *Saloons* | *Estate Cars* |
|---|---|---|
| Length between eye centres, fitted (in): | 47 | 47 |
| Number of leaves: | 4 | 6 |
| Width of leaves (in): | 2 | 2 |
| Thickness of leaves (in): | 3 × 0·230–0·240 | 5 × 0·239–0·249 |
| | 1 × 0·148–0·158 | 1 × 0·370–0·380 |
| Spring camber, fitted (in at lb): | 0·51 at 491–521 | 0·11 at 742–786 |

**Shock-absorbers:** The front shock-absorbers form part of the front suspension unit.

The rear shock-absorbers are double-acting hydraulic telescopic shock-absorbers which require no maintenance.

**Wheel bearings and hubs:** The front wheel hubs are mounted on adjustable taper-roller bearings. When adjusted correctly, the bearings should have neither pre-load nor free play. The rear hubs are flanges forged on to the rear axle shafts. The rear axle shaft outer ends run on non-adjustable ball-bearings.

**Steering gear:** The steering gear is of the worm and nut, recirculating ball type.

*Adjustment:*

Wormshaft end-clearance is adjusted by means of shims and paper gaskets between the steering gear housing and the top cover. Shims are available in thicknesses of 0·004 in and 0·010 in, together with paper gaskets 0·010 in and 0·0025 in thick. Always fit a paper gasket on either side of the shimpack.

First adjust the wormshaft bearings until no clearance can be felt; then remove one 0·004 in shim to slightly pre-load the bearings.

Pitman shaft end-clearance can be corrected by means of shims positioned between the steering gear housing and the top cover plate. For this purpose gaskets of 0·010 in thickness and shims of 0·005 in and 0·010 in are available.

Always fit a paper gasket on either side of the shimpack.

Adjustment is carried out as follows:

Disconnect the steering linkage from the pitman arm.

Check the wormshaft bearings for correct adjustment and correct if necessary.

Remove the steering gear top cover plate and turn the steering wheel to the extreme right or left, until the small hole in the end of the pitman shaft and the hole in the mating cone on the nut are concentric.

The steering gear must always be in this position when checking the pitman shaft pre-load.

Adjust the end-clearance by adding or removing shims until a pre-load of 0·00–0·003 in is obtained.


*Removal:*

Disconnect the battery.

Remove the steering-wheel emblem.

Bend back the locking tab, remove the steering wheel retaining nut and remove the steering wheel.

Pull off the left-hand steering column shroud on right-hand drive cars, or the right-hand shroud on left-hand drive cars, unscrew the four special bolts and remove the other shroud from the column.

Support this shroud away from the column, complete with horn button, direction-indicator and light switches.

It is not necessary to disconnect any wiring.

Remove the parcel shelf.

Remove the cover plate and gasket from the bulkhead.

Remove the bolts securing the mounting clamp to the belt rail and the bolt securing the steering column to the pedal bracket.

On cars equipped with steering column gear-change mechanism, carry out the following operations:

(*a*) Withdraw the pin securing the shift tube to the shifter housing.

(*b*) Withdraw the gear lever and shift tube assembly.

(*c*) At the lower end of the steering column, unscrew the two bolts and spring washers securing the gear-change housing to the steering box.

Jack-up the front of the car and place the car on stands.

Disconnect the steering linkage from the pitman arm, removing the split-pin and unscrewing the castellated nut. Separate the stud from the pitman arm.

Unscrew the three nuts and remove the bolts and flat washers securing the steering gear to the body side-member.

Manoeuvre the steering gear downwards out of the car. Drain the oil.

*Dismantling:*
Mark the pitman shaft and pitman arm, unscrew the pitman arm retaining nut and remove the lock washer. Remove the pitman arm.

Remove from the top cover the small cover plate and gasket.

Remove the two coil springs and thrust button.

Remove the top cover, complete with shimpack and gaskets. (Keep the shim-pack together).

Detach the roller from the peg on the steering nut.

Pull out the pitman shaft.

Remove the bolts securing the steering-column flange to the steering-gear housing, and remove the steering column from the housing.

Remove the spacer.

Unscrew the inner column and withdraw the steering nut complete with thir-teen balls.

Remove the steering shaft upper bearing cup and the twelve bearing balls.

Remove and discard the pitman shaft oil-seal.

Inspect the pitman shaft bushes and, if necessary, renew.

Remove the thirteen balls from the steering nut, inspect all parts for wear and replace those which are unserviceable.

*Reassembling and reinstallation:*
Reassembling is done in the reverse order of removal; special attention should be paid to the following points:

The pitman shaft bushes are not pre-sized and they must be reamed after being pressed into the steering-gear housing.

The pitman shaft oil-seal should be installed with the sharp inner lip facing the bush.

If a new felt bush is fitted in the steering column, it should be soaked for a reasonable period in *hot* heavy grease.

*Specifications:*

| | |
|---|---|
| Steering shaft bearing adjustment: | shims |
| Steering shaft bearing pre-load: | 0·003 in |
| Steering shaft shim thickness and identification: | 0·004 in steel |
| | 0·010 in steel |
| | 0·0025 in paper |
| | 0·010 in paper |
| Pitman shaft bearing adjustment: | shims |
| Pitman shaft pre-load at steering wheel rim: | $1\frac{1}{4}$–$1\frac{1}{2}$ lb |
| Pitman shaft pre-load: | 0·00–0·003 in |
| Pitman shaft shim thickness/identification: | 0·002 in paper |
| | 0·010 in paper |
| | 0·005 in steel |
| | 0·010 in steel |
| Pitman shaft bush diameter (reamed): | 0·812–0·813 in |
| Number of balls in nut: | $13 \times 5/16$ in |
| Number of balls in upper bearing: | $12 \times 7/32$ in |
| in lower bearing: | $12 \times 7/32$ in |

*Tightening torques:*

| | |
|---|---|
| Pitman arm retaining nut: | 60–70 ft lb |
| Steering wheel nut: | 20–25 ft lb |

Steering ball-joints:                               18–22 ft lb
Steering-box top cover to housing:                  12–15 ft lb

**Steering-rod and tie-rods:** The steering-rod and tie-rods are equipped with non-adjustable ball-joints. The tie-rods are adjustable in order to correct toe-in.

**Steering idler arm:** The steering idler arm is supported by means of an idler-arm support bracket and stud; the idler-arm bearing is non-adjustable.

**Steering swivels:** See under *Front suspension.*

**Brakes:** Hydraulically-operated footbrake on all four wheels.
  Mechanically-operated parking brake on rear wheels only.

  The front brakes are of the two-leading-shoe type with a separate cylinder for each brake shoe; the rear brakes have a single-acting cylinder for both shoes; this cylinder also incorporates a mechanical expander, operated by the parking brake lever.

  Each front brake shoe is attached to its brake backing plate by means of a hold-down spindle and spring and one retracting spring.

  Each pair of rear brake shoes is equipped with two retracting springs which must be installed as shown in Figs. 22 and 23, showing the front and rear brake cylinders and related parts.

NOTE: 1965–66 models are fitted with front disc brakes, which are self-adjusting.

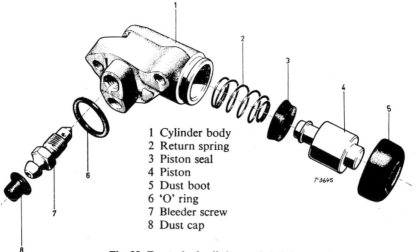

1 Cylinder body
2 Return spring
3 Piston seal
4 Piston
5 Dust boot
6 'O' ring
7 Bleeder screw
8 Dust cap

**Fig. 22. Front wheel cylinder, exploded view**

*Specifications:*

| | |
|---|---|
| Master cylinder bore: | 0·625 in |
| *Front brakes*, drum diameter: | 8·00 in |
| lining, length: | 6·26 in |
| width: | 1·75 in |
| thickness: | 0·187 in |
| area: | 43·98 sq in |
| Wheel cylinder bore: | 0·75 in |

| | |
|---|---|
| *Rear brakes,* drum diameter: | 8·00 in |
| lining, length: | 6·26 in |
| width: | 1·5 in |
| thickness: | 0·188 in |
| area: | 37·70 sq in |
| Wheel cylinder diameter: | 0·75 in |

*Braking ratios and data:*

| | |
|---|---|
| Pedal ratio: | 4 : 1 |
| Hydraulic ratio: | 1·44 : 1 |
| Parking brake ratio, dash mounted: | 4·95 : 1 |
| floor mounted: | 4·85 : 1 |
| Overall ratio, dash-mounted: | 57·62 : 1 |
| floor-mounted: | 56·22 : 1 |
| Pedal travel, to floor pan: | 5·18 in |
| to floor covering: | 5·00 in |
| Parking brake lever travel: | 5·00 in |

*Tightening torques:*

| | |
|---|---|
| Front backing plate to spindle body: | 18–22 ft lb |
| Rear backing plate to axle housing: | 15–18 ft lb |
| Hydraulic unions: | 7–8 ft lb |
| Bleed valves: | 5–7½ ft lb |
| Wheel nuts: | 50–55 ft lb |
| Front wheel cylinders to backing plate: | 4–5 ft lb |
| Rear brake adjuster to backing plate: | 4–5 ft lb |

**Brake adjustment:**

*Front brakes (drum type):*
Each front brake is equipped with two square-headed adjusters. To adjust, proceed as follows:
    Jack-up the front wheel. Turn one brake-shoe adjuster clockwise until the drum is locked. Slowly turn the adjuster anti-clockwise until the drum is free to rotate without drag.
    Adjust the second brake shoe in the same way.

*Rear brakes:*
Each rear brake is equipped with an adjuster unit. Each brake shoe is held in contact with its brake backing-plate thrust pads by means of a single-coil spring.
    The return springs are of unequal length.
    To adjust the rear brakes, proceed as follows:
    Turn the square-headed adjuster clockwise until both shoes are tight against the brake drum, then turn back the adjuster so many 'clicks' that the wheel turns freely.

**Parking brake:** Usually, once the brake shoes are properly adjusted, the parking brake linkage will not need adjustment.
    If, however, an adjustment on the parking brake linkage is necessary, this should be done as follows:
    Check that no sharp bends exist in the handbrake cable.
    Examine the operating levers on the brake backing plate.
    Make sure that each rear wheel expander slides freely in the slots.
    Check the clevis pin and renew where necessary.

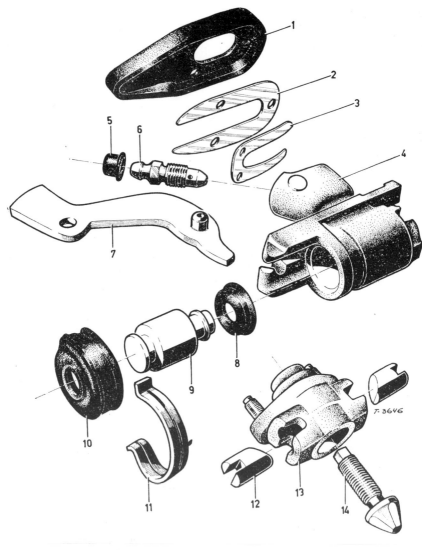

| | |
|---|---|
| 1 Dust boot | 8 Piston seal |
| 2 Retainer | 9 Piston |
| 3 Retainer spring | 10 Dust boot |
| 4 Wheel cylinder | 11 Boot retainer |
| 5 Dust cap | 12 Adjuster |
| 6 Bleed valve | 13 Adjuster body |
| 7 Handbrake lever | 14 Adjuster bolt |

**Fig. 23. Rear wheel cylinder, exploded view**

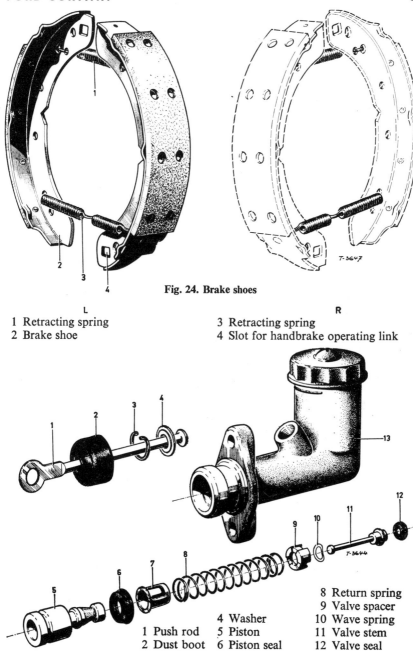

Fig. 24. Brake shoes

L
1 Retracting spring
2 Brake shoe

R
3 Retracting spring
4 Slot for handbrake operating link

| | |
|---|---|
| 1 Push rod | 4 Washer | 8 Return spring |
| 2 Dust boot | 5 Piston | 9 Valve spacer |
| 3 Circlip | 6 Piston seal | 10 Wave spring |
| | 7 Spring retainer | 11 Valve stem |
| | | 12 Valve seal |
| | | 13 Reservoir |

1 Push rod   4 Washer   8 Return spring
2 Dust boot   5 Piston   9 Valve spacer
3 Circlip   6 Piston seal   10 Wave spring
     7 Spring retainer   11 Valve stem
      12 Valve seal
      13 Reservoir

Fig. 25. Brake master cylinder, exploded view

*Adjustment:*
(1) Release the parking brake lever.
(2) Turn the square-headed adjusters clockwise to lock the rear drums.
(3) Slacken the locknut on the adjusting sleeve on the brake cable outer conduit, located in the propeller-shaft tunnel.
    Tighten the nut until all play is taken out of the parking brake cable, then tighten the locknut.
(4) Turn the square-headed adjuster backwards until the drums rotate freely.
(5) Apply the parking brake lever four to five 'clicks'; the brakes should now hold.
(6) Check all split-pins and clevis pins for correct fitting.

**Brake master cylinder:** The brake master cylinder is mounted on the bulkhead in front of the pedal. The brake master cylinder incorporates the brake fluid reservoir.

**Wheels and tyres:** Pressed-steel disc wheels with wide-base rims.

| | |
|---|---|
| Tyres, standard: | 5·20—13 (4-ply) |
| optional: | 5·60—13 (4-ply) |
| Pressures (front and rear): | see page 13 |

For sustained high-speed driving, increase pressures slightly.

## ELECTRICAL EQUIPMENT

**Electrical system:** 12-volt, positive (+) terminal connected to earth.

| | |
|---|---|
| **Battery:** Capacity, standard: | 38 Ah |
| optional: | 51 Ah |
| Plates per cell, standard: | 9 |
| optional: | 11 |
| Specific gravity, charged: | 1·270–1·285 |
| Low limit while discharging at 20-hour rate: | 1·105 |
| Electrolyte capacity, standard: | 4·5 Imp pints |
| optional: | 6·4 Imp pints |
| **Generator:** | 12 V, two-brush |
| Brush length: | 0·718 in |
| **Control box:** Cut-out | |
| cut-in voltage: | 12·6–13·4 V |
| drop-off voltage: | 9·3–11·2 V |
| Armature to core air gap: | 0·035–0·045 in |
| 'Follow-through' of moving contact: | 0·010–0·020 in |
| Current regulator, on-load setting: | maximum generator output, plus or minus 1·5 A |
| Armature to core air gap: | 0·045–0·049 in |
| Voltage regulator, open-circuit setting: | 14·2–14·8 V at 20°C at 1500 rpm |
| Armature to core air gap: | 0·045–0·049 in |

**Temperature correction table:**

| Temperature | Setting voltage |
|---|---|
| 0°C (32°F) | 14·6–15·2 |
| 10°C (50°F) | 14·4–15·0 |

| 20°C (68°F) | 14·2–14·8 |
| 30°C (86°F) | 14·0–14·6 |
| 40°C (104°F) | 13·8–14·4 |

Resistance of shunt windings:
    cut-out                                8·8–9·6 Ohm
    voltage regulator:               10·8–12·0 Ohm

'Swamp' resistor:
    resistance measured between centre tag
        and base:                     13·25–14·25 Ohm
    resistance measured between tags ends
        before fitting:              53–57 Ohm

Field resistor:                     55–65 Ohm (red) or 37–43 Ohm (yellow) depending on type of control box.

Relationship between control box, generator and battery:

| | Control box | Generator | Battery |
|---|---|---|---|
| Standard: | Part No. 622E–10505–A | Part No. 105E–10001–B | |
| | Identification No. 37344 | Identification No. C40 | |
| | (on base of control box) | Rated output 22A | 38Ah |
| Optional: | Part No. 622E–10505–B | Part No. 109E–10001 | |
| | Identification No. 37342 | Identification No. C40L | |
| | (on base of control box) | Rated output 25A | 51Ah |

**Starter motor:** Type:             12V, 4-pole
Number of brushes:             four (two earthed)
Current draw, zero rpm:        340A at 7·4V
                 1000 rpm:     245A at 8·7V
Lock torque:                   6·4 ft lb
Number of teeth on ring gear:    110
Number of teeth on pinion:       nine
Gear ratio:                    12·22 : 1
Commutator end bearing bush:
    length:                   0·495–0·505 in
    inside diameter:         0·4995–0·5005 in
    outside diameter:      0·6235–0·6245 in
Drive end bearing bush:
    length:                   0·68875–0·71875 in
    inside diameter:         0·7495–0·7505 in
    outside diameter:      0·812–0·813 in

**Bulbs:**                       *Wattage*
Sealed-beam units:           60/45
Side lights and front direction-indicator:   6/21
Rear direction-indicator:      21
Tail/stoplight:               6/21
Rear number plate light:      6
Interior light:               3
Instrument panel light:       2·2

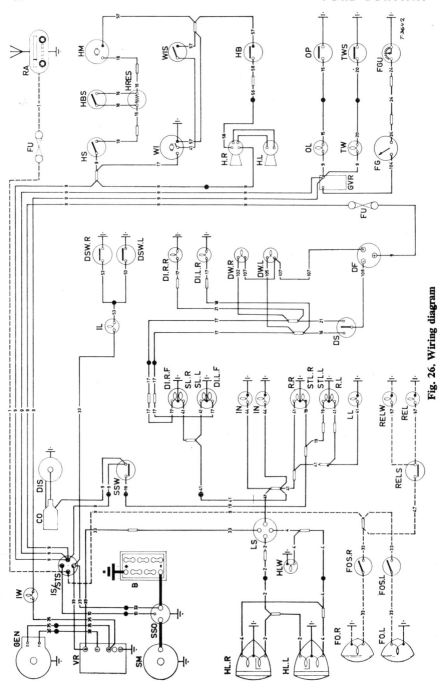

**Fig. 26, Wiring diagram**

*Key to Fig.* 26:

| | | | |
|---|---|---|---|
| B | Battery | HRES | Heater motor resistance |
| CO | Coil | HS | Heater Motor switch |
| DF | Direction-indicator flasher unit | IL. | Interior light |
| DI.L.F. | Direction-indicator, left front | IN. | Instrument light |
| DI.R.F. | Direction-indicator, right front | IS/STS | Ignition/starter switch |
| DI.L.R. | Direction-indicator, left rear | IW. | Ignition/generator warning |
| DI.R.R. | Direction-indicator, right rear | | light |
| DIS | Distributor | LL | Number plate light |
| DS | Direction-indicator switch | LS | Light switch |
| DSW.L. | Door switch, left | OL. | Oil pressure warning light |
| DSW.R. | Door switch, right | OP | Oil pressure switch |
| DW.L. | Direction-indicator warning | R.R. | Rearlamp, right |
| | light, left | R.L. | Rearlamp, left |
| DW.R. | Direction-indicator warning | RA. | Radio (optional) |
| | light, right | REL | Reverse lamp |
| FG | Fuel gauge | RELS. | Reverse lamp switch |
| FGU. | Fuel gauge tank unit | RELW | Reverse lamp warning light |
| FO.L. | Foglamp, left | SL.L. | Sidelamp, left |
| FO.R. | Foglamp, right | SL.R. | Sidelamp, right |
| FOS.L. | Foglamp switch, left | SM | Starter motor |
| FOS.R. | Foglamp switch, right | SSO. | Starter solenoid |
| FU | Fuses | SSW. | Stoplamp switch |
| GEN. | Generator | STL.L. | Stoplamp, left |
| GVR. | Gauge voltage regulator | STL.R. | Stoplamp, right |
| H.L. | Horn, left | TW. | Water temperature warning |
| H.R. | Horn, right | | light |
| HB. | Horn button | TWS | Water temperature warning |
| HBS. | Heater booster switch | | light switch |
| HL.L. | Headlamp, left | VR | Voltage regulator |
| HL.R. | Headlamp, right | WI. | Windscreen wiper |
| HLW. | Main beam warning light | WIS. | Windscreen wiper switch. |
| HM. | Heater motor | | |

*Key to wire colours, Fig.* 26:

| | | | |
|---|---|---|---|
| 2 | Blue/red | 35 | Brown/yellow |
| 4 | Blue/white | 38 | Brown/green |
| 9 | White | 41 | Red |
| 10 | White/red | 44 | Red/white |
| 15 | White/brown | 47 | Red/brown |
| 16 | White/black | 53 | Purple/white |
| 17 | Green | 57 | Black |
| 19 | Green/yellow | 102 | Light green/red |
| 20 | Green/blue | 104 | Light green/blue |
| 24 | Green/black | 107 | Light green/purple |
| 33 | Brown | 108 | Light green/brown |

# FORD CORTINA G.T.

The G.T. version of the Cortina Super was introduced in April, 1963, designation 118E G.T. (l.h.d.: 119E G.T.) in two- and four-door Saloon versions. The engine is a modified version of the 1498cc unit, with twin-choke Weber carburettor. Standard equipment includes floor-mounted gear change with centre console, improved interior trim, extra instrumentation (including oil pressure gauge, rev. counter, and ammeter), disc brakes at front, larger rear brakes, and G.T. badges on rear quarter panels. 1965 models are fitted with twin radius arms to the rear suspension, as a result of competition experience, and a new facia (for other modifications and prices, see Cortina 1200 and 1500). The technical specification differs from that of the Cortina Super mainly in the following respects:

## ENGINE

| | |
|---|---|
| Maximum bhp: | 83·5 (gross) 78 (net) at 5200 rpm |
| Maximum torque: | 97 lb ft (gross) 91 lb ft (net) at 3600 rpm |
| Maximum bmep: | 150 lb/sq in at 3600 rpm |
| Piston clearance in bore: | 0·0011 to 0·0017 in |
| Valve head diameter: | inlet, 1·410 in; exhaust, 1·245 in |
| Valve lift: | inlet, 0·3420 in; exhaust, 0·3367 in |
| Valve timing, inlet: | opens 27° B.T.D.C., closes 65° A.B.D.C. |
| exhaust: | opens 65° B.B.D.C., closes 27° A.T.D.C. |
| Valve clearance, hot: | inlet 0·014 in, exhaust 0·021 in |
| cold: | inlet 0·012 in, exhaust 0·022 in |

Fig. 27. Cortina G.T. 1965, front compartment

| | | |
|---|---|---|
| Ignition timing: | | 10° B.T.D.C. |
| Spark plugs: | | 1963–64: Champion N4 or Autolite AG2; |
| | | 1965–66: Autolite AG22 |
| Vacuum advance (crankshaft | | |
| degrees) | starts at: | 6·0in Hg |
| | maximum: | 24° at 17in Hg |
| Centrifugal advance (crankshaft rpm | | |
| and degrees): | starts at: | 1200rpm |
| | maximum: | 36° at 5500rpm |
| Carburettor: | | Weber twin-choke compound |
| Type: | | 1963–64:  28/36 DCD 16/18 |
| | | 1965–66:  28/36 DCD 22 |

| | *Primary* | *Secondary* |
|---|---|---|
| Choke tube diameter: | 26mm | 27mm |
| Main jet: | 140 | 155 |
| Compensating jet: | 230 | 180 |
| Idling jet: | 50 | 70 |
| Idling jet air bleed: | 200 | 70 |
| Emulsion tube: | F30 | F30 |
| Accelerator pump jet: | 60 | |
| Starter jet: | 190 | |
| Starter jet air bleed: | 100 | |
| Float needle valve: | 1·75mm | |

## BRAKES

| | |
|---|---|
| Type, front: | Girling 9·5in diameter discs |
| rear: | Girling 9·0in diameter drums |
| Rear brake linings: | Don 24 (8·61 × 1·70 × 0·187in) |

## FRONT SUSPENSION

| | |
|---|---|
| Type: | i.f.s., coil springs (6·71 coils) |
| Wire diameter: | 0·501–0·507in |
| Spring length: | free, 10in; loaded, 6·27in (at 552lb) |
| Spring rate: | 135–146lb/in |

## REAR SUSPENSION

| | |
|---|---|
| Type: | Semi-elliptic leaf springs |
| | (1965–66: with twin radius arms) |
| Number of leaves: | 5 (1963–4), 4 (1965) |
| Thickness of leaves: | 1 × 0·235–0·245in ⎫ |
| | 3 × 0·220–0·230in ⎬ 1963–4 |
| | 1 × 0·300–0·310in ⎭ |
| | 2 × 0·235–0·245in ⎫ |
| | 2 × 0·220–0·230in ⎬ 1965 |
| Width of leaves: | 2·0in |
| Spring camber, fitted: | 0·26in at 488–518lb |

## TYRE PRESSURES (cold)

| | |
|---|---|
| 1963-64: | front, 22lb/sq in; rear, 24lb/sq in |
| 1965–66: | 24–30lb/sq in, according to speed |

# FORD CORTINA-LOTUS

The 'Cortina developed by Lotus' is a much modified two-door saloon, bearing designation 125E, Series LP, body code 74. It was introduced in January 1963, fitted with the Lotus version of the 1½-litre Ford engine, incorporating twin overhead camshafts and aluminium cylinder head, short, remote control gear change, suspension specially developed for high speeds, power-assisted front brakes, wide-base rim wheels with special tyres, etc. For prices of this model see under *Cortina*.

Listed below are brief specifications and adjustment data.

This model was replaced by the Mk. II version in March 1967.

## ENGINE

| | |
|---|---|
| Type: | 4-cylinder, twin-ohc |
| Bore × stroke: | 82·55 × 72·746 mm |
| Cubic capacity: | 1558 cc |
| Compression ratio: | 9·5 : 1 |
| Maximum bhp: | 105 (net) at 5500 rpm |
| Maximum torque: | 108 lb ft at 4000 rpm |
| Maximum bmep: | 171·4 lb/sq in at 4000 rpm |
| Compression pressure: | 170 lb/sq in at cranking speed |
| Valve timing, inlet: | opens 22° B.T.D.C.; closes 62° A.T.D.C. |
| exhaust: | opens 62° B.B.D.C.; closes 22° A.T.D.C. |
| Valve clearance (cold): | 0·005–0·006 in inlet; 0·006–0·007 in exhaust |
| Oil pressure: | 35–40 lb/sq in |
| Ignition timing: | 14° B.T.D.C. (approx.) |
| Spark plugs: | 1963–64, Lodge 2 HLN; 1965–66, Autolite AG22 |

**Fig. 28. Cortina-Lotus Saloon (1965-66 model shown)**

Spark plug gap:                                             0·023–0·027 in
Contact-breaker points gap:                                0·014–0·016 in
Centrifugal advance (crankshaft rpm
    and degrees)    starts at:     2000 rpm
                maximum:   38° at 6500 rpm
Carburettors:                                              two, Weber twin-choke compound
  Type:                                                    40 DCOE/18, horizontal
  Choke tube diameter:                                     main 30, auxiliary 4·5
  Main jet:                                                115
  Compensating jet:                                        200
  Idling jet:                                              F9/45
  Starter jet:                                             F5/100
  Starter jet air bleed:                                   100
  Emulsion tube:                                           F11
  Accelerator pump jet:                                    40
  Accelerator pump inlet valve
    bleed:                                                 50
  Pump spring length:                                      20·5 mm (with 110 grams load)
  Progression holes:                                       $1 \times 120$, $2 \times 100$
  Needle valve:                                            1·75 mm
  Float weight:                                            26 grams
  Float level:                                             8·5 mm (including gasket)
  Fuel level:                                              29 mm
Cylinder-head bolt tightening
  torque:                                                  60 lb ft
Cylinder-head bolt tightening
  sequence:

| front: | 9 | 3 | 1 | 5 | 7 |
|---|---|---|---|---|---|
|  | 8 | 6 | 2 | 4 | 10 |

## BRAKES

Type, front:                   Girling 9·5 in diameter discs
    rear:              Girling 9·0 in diameter drums
Servo:                         suspended vacuum type
Rear linings:                  8·28 × 1·75 in

## FRONT SUSPENSION

Type:                          i.f.s., coil springs
Number of coils:               7·07–7·31
Wire diameter:                 0·466–0·472 in
Spring length:                 free, 11·75 in; loaded, 6·33 in (at 488–510 lb)
Spring deflection rate:        91–99 lb/in

## FRONT WHEEL ALIGNMENT

Castor (kerb weight):          0° 36′ negative
Camber (kerb weight):          0° 40′
KPI (kerb weight):             5° 54′
Toe-in (at wheel rim):         $\frac{1}{16}$–$\frac{1}{8}$ in

## REAR SUSPENSION

Type:                                coil springs; 'A' bracket for axle location, and
                                     twin radius arms (from September 1965:
                                     semi-elliptic leaf springs)
Number of coils:                     14·9
Wire diameter:                       0·379–0·385 in
Spring length:                       free, 14·33 in; loaded, 9·25 in (at 540–560 lb)
Spring deflection rate:              108 lb/in

## TRANSMISSION

Standard final drive ratio:          3·90 : 1
Overall gear ratios, first:          9·750 : 1 (g/b 2·50 : 1)
                  second:            6·396 : 1 (g/b 1·64 : 1)
                  third:             4·797 : 1 (g/b 1·23 : 1)
                  top:               3·900 : 1 (g/b 1·00 : 1)
                  reverse:           10·959 : 1 (g/b 2·81 : 1)
Alternative gearbox ratios:          on application
Alternative final drive ratios:      3·77 : 1, 4·1 : 1, 4·43 : 1
NOTE: From October 1965 fitted with Corsair V4 GT type close-ratio gearbox.

## WHEELS AND TYRES

Wheels:                              13 × 5½J, wide base ring
Tyres:                               6·00–13 tubeless nylon speed

## TYRE PRESSURES (Cold)

Normal, front and rear:              20 lb/sq in
High speeds:                         22 lb/sq in (front), 27 lb/sq in (rear)

## CAPACITIES AND LUBRICANTS

Engine sump (including filter):      6¼ Imp pints
Engine lubricant, above 0°C:         SAE 20W
                  below 0°C:         SAE 10W
Gearbox:                             1¾ Imp pints
Gearbox lubricant:                   SAE 80 EP
Rear axle:                           2 Imp pints
Rear axle lubricant:                 SAE 90 EP (for topping-up only)
Steering box:                        ⅔ Imp pint
Steering box lubricant:              SAE 90 EP
Cooling system:                      10¼ Imp pints
Fuel tank:                           8 Imp gallons

## DIMENSIONS

|                        | inches  |
|------------------------|---------|
| Wheelbase:             | 98·4    |
| Overall length:        | 168·3   |
| width:                 | 62·5    |
| height:                | 53·9    |
| Track, front:          | 51·6    |
| rear:                  | 50·2    |
| Ground clearance:      | 5·3     |
| Turning circle:        | 34 ft   |

# GENERAL FAULT FINDING CHART
## FOR PETROL ENGINES

Some items in this chart are not applicable to *every* make of petrol engine

## Engine will not start

**A. Starter does not crank engine**

| | |
|---|---|
| Battery run down | *Recharge; replace if defective* |
| Battery posts and terminals loose or corroded | *Clean and tighten. If badly corroded, soak with water to facilitate removal and avoid damage to the battery posts* |
| Faulty starter switch or solenoid, if fitted; broken battery cable or loose connection | *Check wires and cables; check solenoid and switch, replace if defective* |
| Starter motor defective | *Repair or replace* |
| Starter drive stuck (starter will run, but does not crank engine) | *Clean and if necessary repair or replace* |
| Starter drive pinion jammed with starter ring gear | *Free by rotating squared end of starter spindle with a spanner* |

**B. Starter cranks engine slowly**

| | |
|---|---|
| Battery partly run down | *Recharge; replace if defective* |
| Loose or corroded connections | *Clean and tighten* |
| Faulty starter switch or solenoid; partly broken cable or loose connection | *Check wires and cables; check solenoid and switch, replace if necessary* |
| Starter motor defective | *Repair or replace* |

**C. Starter cranks engine, but engine will not start**

*Trouble in ignition system:*

*No spark at plugs:*

| | |
|---|---|
| Moisture on spark plugs, ignition distributor, coil and wires (this trouble often occurs after parking overnight in foggy or rainy weather) | *Clean and dry. Avoid recurrence by coating wires, distributor rotor, cap, coil and spark plug insulators with moisture-proof lacquer* |
| Spark plugs flooded, due to excessive use of choke | *Start engine on full throttle. If this does not help, clean plugs. With plugs removed, turn over the crankshaft a few times to blow the accumulated fuel from the cylinders* |

| | |
|---|---|
| Spark plugs oiled up | *Clean; if necessary replace* |
| Spark plug insulator cracked | *Replace* |
| Spark plug gap too wide or too close | *Reset gap* |
| *No Spark at distributor:* | |
| Loose, broken or shorted low-tension lead between coil and/or inside distributor | *Check and tighten; also check internal leads in distributor. These leads sometimes break inside their insulation, and the break is not always visible. Pull carefully on one end; a broken lead will stretch* |
| Cracked rotor or distributor cap | *Replace* |
| Contact breaker points dirty, worn or maladjusted | *Clean and adjust; if necessary replace* |
| Carbon brush in distributor cap not making contact | *Free; if necessary replace* |
| Faulty condenser | *Replace* |
| *No spark at coil:* | |
| High tension lead loose or broken | *Replace* |
| Broken or loose low-tension leads or faulty ignition switch | *Check wiring, repair or replace; check switch, replace if defective* |

| | |
|---|---|
| **D. Starter cranks engine, but engine will not start** | |
| *Trouble in fuel system:* | |
| *No petrol in carburettor:* | |
| Empty fuel tank | *Fill-up. If necessary, check and repair or replace fuel gauge* |
| Obstructed or damaged fuel pipe | *Clean; if necessary repair or replace* |
| Air leak in petrol line | *Check and repair or replace. Pay special attention to flexible fuel line (if fitted). If flexible fuel line is porous, a temporary 'get-you-home' repair can often be made by securely wrapping the line with friction tape or rubbing with hard soap* |
| Fuel filter clogged | *Clean and refit with new gasket. Always carry a spare gasket and a glass filter bowl, if so equipped* |

| | |
|---|---|
| Fuel pump defective | *Repair or replace. If electric pump does not function, lightly tap pump housing until ticking resumes* |
| *Petrol in carburettor:* | |
| Jets clogged | *Clean; blow out with air (never use wire to clean jets)* |
| Float needle stuck | *Clean or replace* |
| Carburettor flooded | *Clean float needle valve; if necessary replace. If this trouble persists, check fuel pump pressure* |
| Choke control faulty | *Repair or replace* |
| Air leak at inlet manifold or carburettor base | *Check nuts and bolts for tightness; if necessary replace gaskets* |
| Water or dirt in carburettor | *Clean. If this trouble persists, check rubber hose in fuel tank filler neck for damage or looseness, causing water to enter tank* |

NOTE: *If ignition system and carburettor are in order, yet the engine will not start, check timing*

## Engine starts but does not run properly

| | |
|---|---|
| **E. Engine misfires** | |
| *Ignition trouble* | |
| Spark plug or coil leads loose or damaged | *Tighten; replace if necessary* |
| Incorrect spark plug gap | *Regap* |
| Cracked spark plug insulator | *Replace faulty spark plug* |
| Spark plug oiled up | *Clean, if necessary replace with spark plug of correct type. If trouble persists, check for mechanical trouble* |
| Cracked distributor cap | *Replace* |
| Loose connection in primary circuit | *Check and repair. Also check, and if necessary replace, ignition switch. In rare cases the ammeter has been found to be the cause of this trouble, due to faulty internal connection* |
| Distributor otherwise faulty | *See* **C** |
| *Trouble in fuel system* | *See* **D** |

*Mechanical trouble*

| | |
|---|---|
| Incorrect valve clearance | *Adjust* |
| Valve sticking | *Try to free by pouring a gum solvent of good quality into carburettor air intake; if not successful, dismantle and repair* |
| Valve spring broken | *Replace. Usually the valve concerned will have to be ground* |
| Worn piston, piston rings and cylinder or burnt valve; cylinder-head gasket blown | *Test compression; if too low, dismantle for repairs* |

**F. Engine starts and stops**

| | |
|---|---|
| *Trouble in ignition or fuel system:* | *See* **C** *and* **D** |
| Obstructed exhaust system | *Check and repair or replace* |

**G. Engine runs on wide throttle only**

| | |
|---|---|
| Idle jet clogged or mixture improperly adjusted | *Clean idle jet and/or idle air bleed; adjust* |
| Valve sticking or burnt; valve spring broken; other mechanical trouble | *Check and repair. Pay special attention to heat riser, if so equipped, since a burnt heat riser tube will cause exhaust gas to enter intake manifold. This will sometimes cause backfiring in carburettor* |

**H. Lack of power**

| | |
|---|---|
| Ignition too far retarded or other ignition trouble | *Check and correct (See* **C***)* |
| Obstructed exhaust system | *Dented exhaust pipe and/or muffler Dislocated baffle plate or muffler Replace* |
| Trouble in fuel system | *Check and correct (See* **D***)* |
| Loss of compression | *Test compression; if found to be too low, check valve clearance. If valve clearance is properly adjusted and compression is still low, check for other mechanical trouble, such as burnt valves and/or worn pistons, rings and cylinders* |
| Dragging brakes | *Check and correct. Essentially this is not an engine trouble* |

**I. Engine runs roughly**

| | |
|---|---|
| Ignition timing incorrect | *Check and correct. Pay attention to possibly stuck advance mechanism, because the fixed advance may be correctly adjusted, yet the timing while running will be incorrect if the automatic advance is stuck* |
| Lean or rich mixture | *Check carburettor and fuel system, see* **D** |
| Improperly adjusted valve clearance | *Check and correct* |

**J. Engine knocks**

| | |
|---|---|
| Ignition too far advanced | *Check and correct. Attend to possibly stuck advance mechanism, see* **I** |
| Excessive carbon deposit | *Decarbonize* |
| Loose bearings or pistons or other mechanical cause | *Check and repair* |

**K. Engine overheats**

*Cooling system:*

| | |
|---|---|
| Lack of water | *Top-up and check for leaks* |
| Fan belt loose or broken | *Check and adjust or replace* |
| Radiator clogged by insects | *Clean* |
| Cooling system clogged internally (in water-cooled engines) | *Clean with a cooling system cleaner of a reputable make and flush out according to maker's instructions. Inspect radiator hoses and replace if in bad condition* |
| Thermostat stuck or faulty | *Check and replace if necessary* |
| Ignition improperly timed | *Check and correct. Attend to possibly stuck advance mechanism* |
| Lean or rich mixture | *Check fuel system; see* **D** |
| Excessive carbon deposit | *Decarbonize* |
| Obstructed exhaust system | *Check and repair or replace* |
| Cylinder-head gasket of the incorrect type | *Replace* |

# INDEX

# The jam buster.

Now with the help of this manual you probably have your car in perfect running order – but what use is it to you if you have to spend your time in one long traffic queue? To beat the traffic you must have *The Sunday Times RAC Road Atlas* with its special guide on how to get round Britain's most notorious traffic jams. The following are just some of its special advantages.

- **New road classification numbers**
- **93 pages of maps based on the famous Mobil 5 miles-to-the inch road system**
- **Complete London section plus comprehensive tourist guide**
- **Gazetteer describing over 3000 towns and villages**
- **100 brand new town plans – based on 4 years research by the R.A.C.**
- **Colour guide to the latest traffic signs**
- **Beat the traffic guide**
- **12 ways to get you home. A new illustrated guide on how to cope with a breakdown.**

$11\frac{1}{4}$" $\times$ $7\frac{3}{4}$", 304 pp, 93 pp full-colour maps, 5 miles to the inch, 300 places described in Gazetteer, 100 new Townplans, 25000 name index – and much more for only 63s

'For me this new Road Atlas has become an indispensable part of the interior fittings of my car.' *Good Housekeeping*

**BUY YOUR COPY FROM A BOOKSHOP NOW**
or if in difficulty write to Thomas Nelson & Sons, 36 Park Street, London W1Y 4DE